Napkin Folding

40 IDEAS FOR ORIGINAL TABLE SETTINGS

SEARCH PRESS

First published in Great Britain 2020 by
Search Press Limited
Wellwood, North Farm Road,
Tunbridge Wells, Kent TN2 3DR

© 2012 First published in French as *Pliages de serviettes* by
Editions Marie Claire-Societe d'Information et de Creations (SIC)

English translation by Burravoe Translation Services

Napkin folder and diagram designer: Virginie Rousset
Photographs: Pierre Nicou
Styling: Marie-Paule Faure
Graphic design and layout: Either studio
Cover: Either studio

ISBN 978-1-78221-761-9

Contents

In all
simplicity

Fold it flat

1.

Lay a square (or rectangular) napkin on your work surface, wrong side up. Fold the top quarter of the napkin down to the centre.

2.

Repeat at the bottom of the napkin, folding the bottom quarter up to the centre.

3.

Fold the right and left sides of the napkin inwards, forming folds a few centimetres wide. Starch. Iron to press the folds.

4.

Fold the left-hand edge of the napkin to the right. Leave a strip of fabric uncovered.

5.

Fold the left-hand edge of the napkin to the right again. Ensure that the two folds on the right are the same width. Iron all the folds.

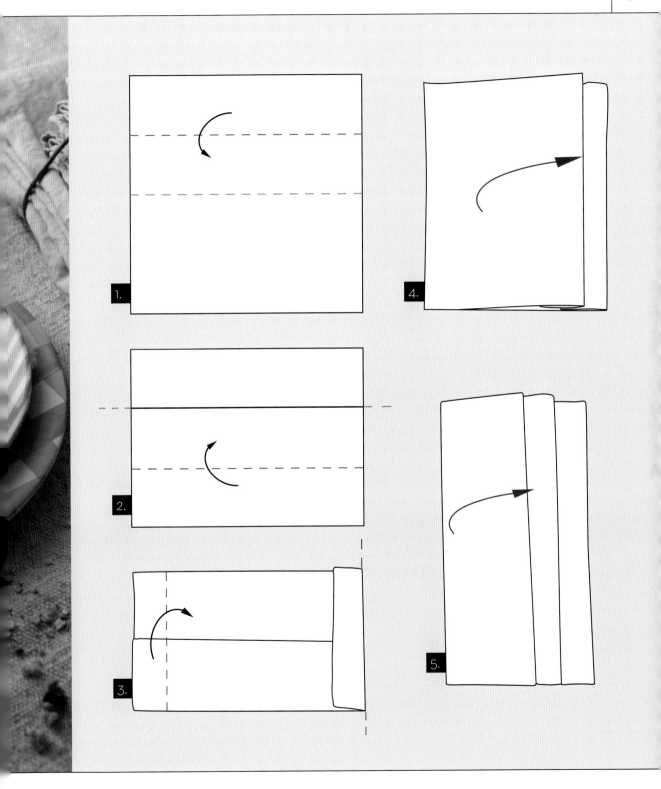

Pretty points

1.

Lay a square napkin on your work surface, right side up. Fold diagonally (point D to point B). Iron to mark the fold. Unfold the napkin. Repeat, folding the napkin to the opposite diagonal (point A to point C). Iron to mark the fold. Unfold. Flip the napkin over (right side down).

2.

Fold the napkin in half horizontally (point C to point B and point D to point A). Iron to mark the fold. Unfold the napkin. Repeat, folding the napkin in half vertically (points A/B to points D/C). Iron to mark the fold. Unfold the napkin.

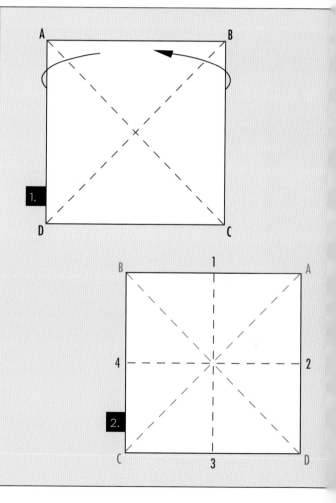

3.

Pinch corner B between the index finger and thumb of your left hand. Do the same for corner C with the index finger and thumb of your right hand. Bring point B to point C by bringing your thumbs together. Point 4 will fold inwards naturally along the crease you ironed in previously. It is now aligned with the centre of the napkin.

4.

Repeat, bringing points A and D together. When all the layers are on top of each other, you are left with a triangle. Spray with starch and iron to press the folds.

5.

Hold the top of the triangle in place with your fingertip. Fold point D towards point C' along the dashed red line. Iron to press this fold.

6.

Keep your finger on the top of the triangle. Fold point A to point D' along the dashed red line. Iron to mark this fold. Flip the napkin over.

7.

Pull point B to the right. The napkin will open out naturally to form a triangle along the crease you marked previously (dashed red line). Spray with starch. Iron. Flip the napkin over.

8.

Fold the last point along the dashed red lines, bringing point B to point A'. Spray with starch. Iron.

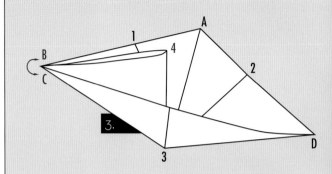

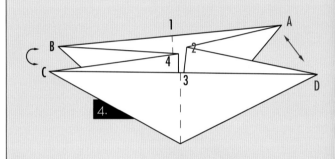

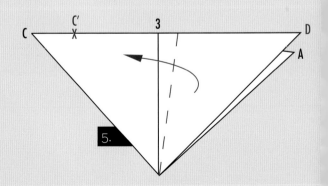

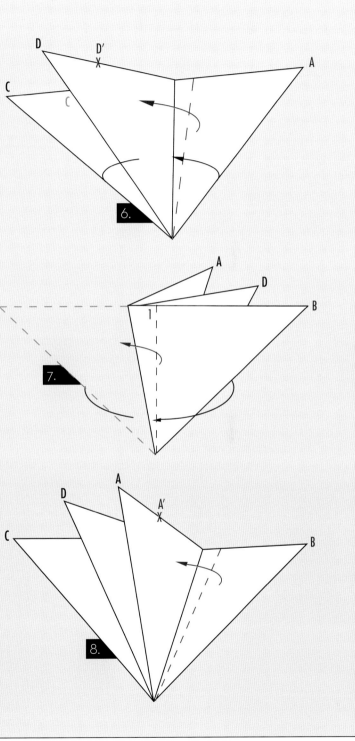

Cutlery pouch

1.
Lay a square napkin on your work surface, right side up.
Fold in half horizontally, along the dashed red line.
Spray lightly with starch.
Iron to press the fold.

2.
Fold this rectangle in half vertically, along the dashed red lines, to form a square. Iron.

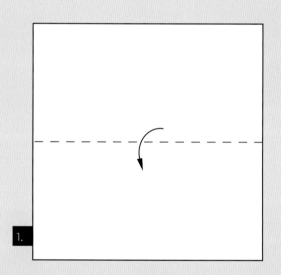

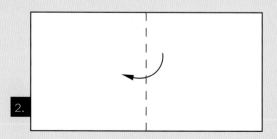

3.
This square now comprises four layers of fabric.
Take hold of the top left corner of the top layer (A).
Fold along the diagonal, bringing point A to point B.

4.
Fold in the right-hand third of the napkin, following
the dashed red line. Iron to press the fold.

5.
Fold in the left-hand third.

6.
Slip the bottom of the left-hand flap into the
fold of the right-hand flap in order to hold the
napkin closed.
Flip the napkin over.

7.
Spray with starch. Iron the folds.
Slip the cutlery, the menu or a table name card into
the pouch that you have made.

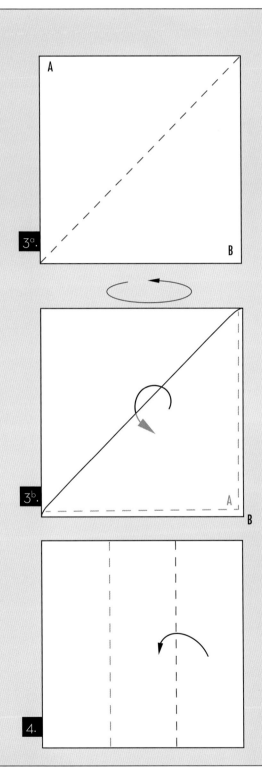

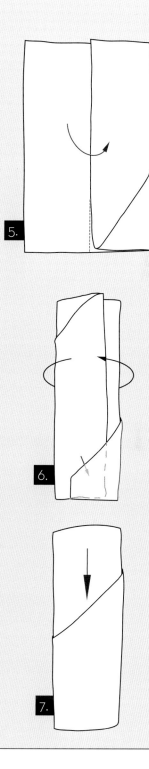

5.

6.

7.

Cravat points

1.
Lay a square napkin on the work surface, wrong side up. Fold in half diagonally, along the dashed red line. Turn the napkin so the point of the triangle is downwards.

2.
Place your finger on point A (located in the middle of the top edge), then fold the right-hand side of the napkin over the left-hand side along the dashed red line.

3.
Fold the shaded part towards the folds on the left.

4.
Adjust the final fold as required. The point should be centred, forming a necktie shape. Spray with starch and iron the folds.

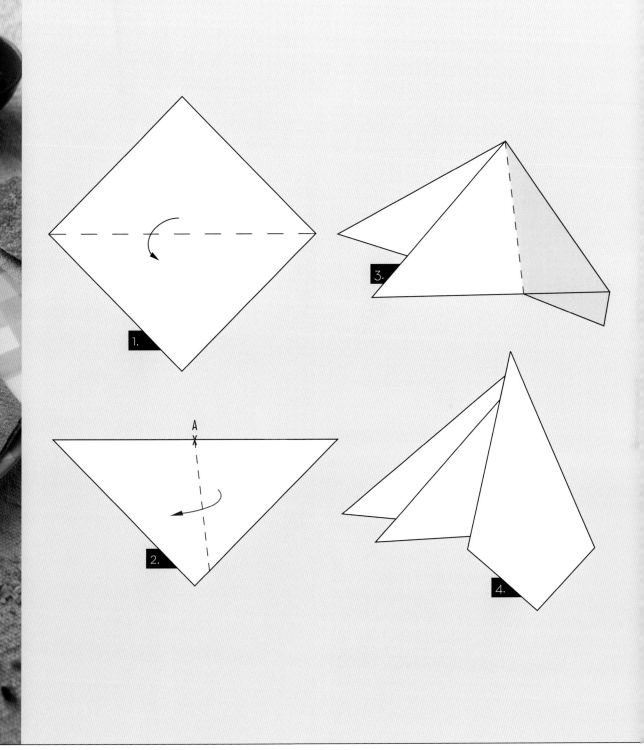

Flat knot

1.
Lay a square (or rectangular) napkin on your work
surface, wrong side up.
Fold in half horizontally.

2.
Fold this rectangle in half horizontally.

3.
Fold the napkin in half horizontally for a third time.
Spray with starch. Iron to give sharp folds.

4.
Fold the right-hand third of the napkin downwards,
forming a right angle.

5.
Holding point A in place with a finger, fold the
left-hand third of the napkin downwards behind,
forming a right angle.

6.
Holding point B in place with one finger, fold the
left-hand section (1) across the front, forming a
right angle.
Section 1 crosses in front of section 2.

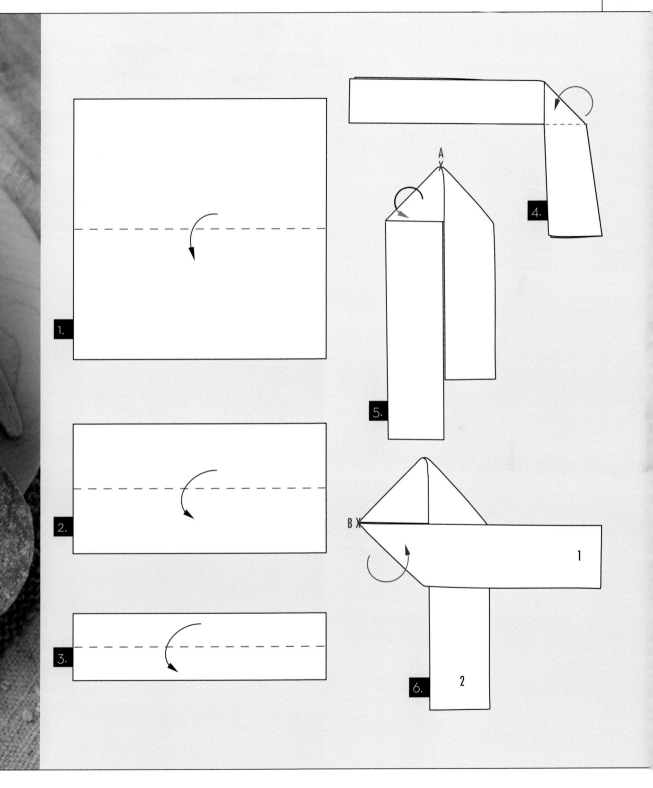

1.

2.

3.

4.

5.

6.

A

B

1

2

All tied up

1.
Lay a square napkin on the work surface, wrong side up.
Fold in half horizontally, along the dashed red line.
Spray lightly with starch.
Iron to press the fold.

2.
Fold this rectangle in half vertically, along the dashed red line, to form a square. Iron.

3.
Fold the right-hand and left-hand thirds of the napkin inwards, placing one under the other.

4.
Wind a length of wool around the folded napkin.
Finish with a simple knot. Flip the napkin over.

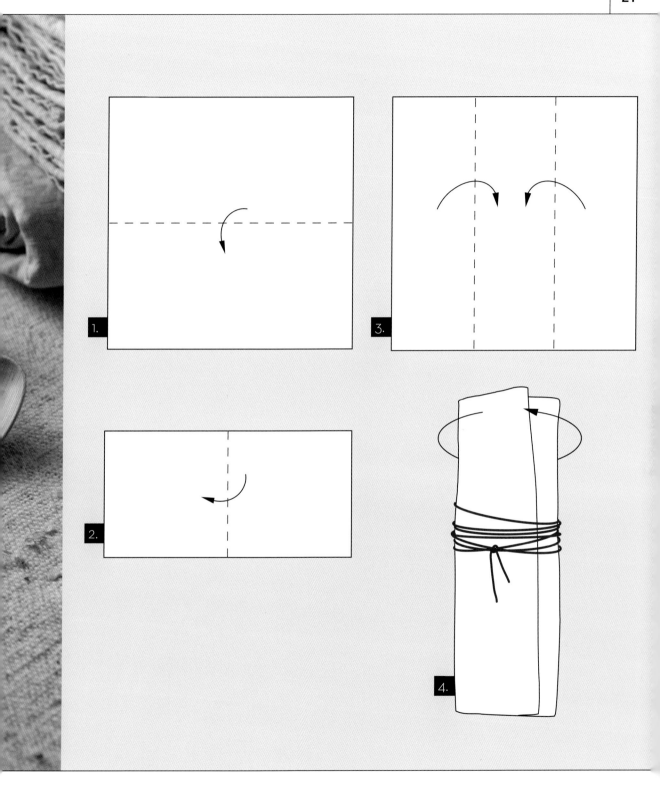

A touch of romance

Chic wallet

1.
Lay a square napkin on your work surface, right side up.
Fold in half horizontally, along the dashed red line.
Spray with starch.
Iron to press the crease.

2.
Fold in half vertically along the dashed red line.

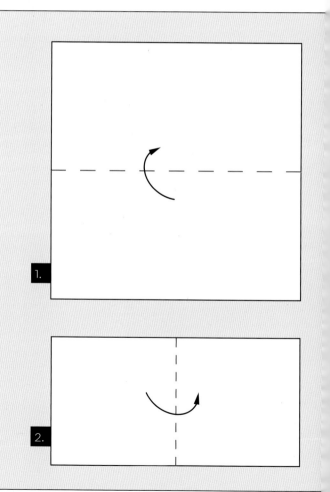

3.

This square now comprises four layers of fabric. Roll the top layer only from the top right-hand corner to the middle of the napkin. Starch, then iron to press the folds.

4.

Tuck the next layer of fabric under the first fold. Leave a strip of fabric of the same width uncovered. Iron.

5.

Tuck the third layer of fabric under the second fold. Leave a strip of the same width uncovered.

6.

Rotate the napkin so the folds run horizontally. Fold the left- and right-hand sides behind. Make sure you keep the points (A and B) centred. Iron.

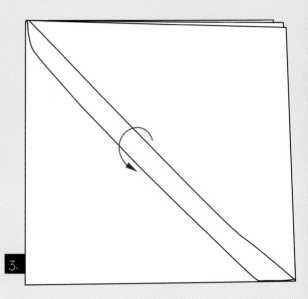

3.

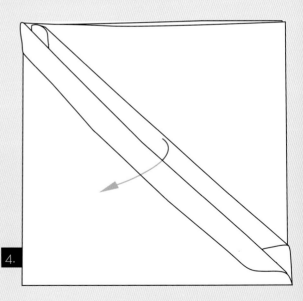

4.

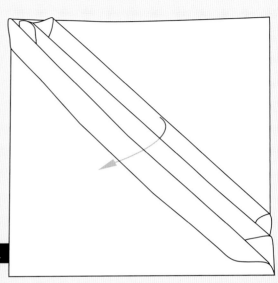

5.

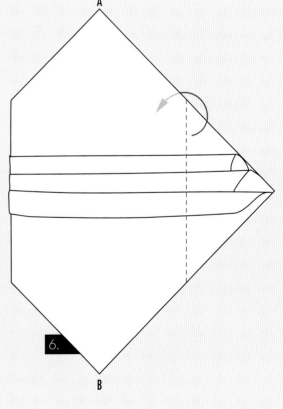

A

B

6.

Precious star

1.

Lay a square napkin on the work surface, wrong side up. Fold in half diagonally. Iron to mark the fold. Unfold. Repeat on the other diagonal. Iron and then unfold.

2.

Fold each corner of the napkin into the centre along the dashed red lines, so that points A, B, C and D meet at point E. Iron the folds. Flip the napkin over.

3.

Repeat the previous step. Fold the corners of the napkin into the centre along the dashed red lines. Iron the folds. Flip the napkin over.

4.

Having flipped the napkin, fold the corners to the centre a final time, following the dashed red lines. Iron the folds.

5.

To form the branches of the star, unfold the triangles of fabric that are underneath each corner.

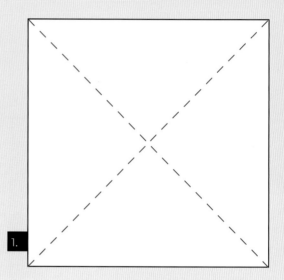

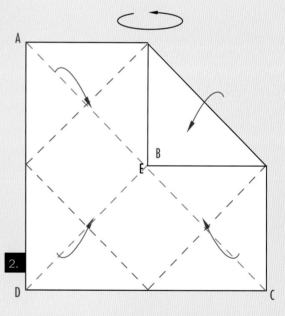

3.

4.

5.

A must-have

1.

If you start with an A4 sheet of paper, the final envelope will measure 13 x 9cm (5 x 3½in). If you start with an A3 sheet, the final wallet will measure 19 x 13cm (7½ x 5in).
Fold the sheet in half horizontally, along the dashed red line. Mark the fold.

2.

Fold the top layer in half horizontally, following the dashed red line.
Align edges A and B.

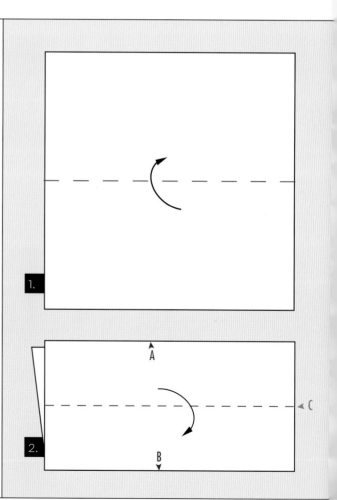

3.
Fold the top layer in half horizontally again. Align edges A and C.
Use your nail to mark the fold, then unfold.

4.
Fold edge A to crease D (which you marked previously) along the dashed red line.

5.
Fold this band (shaded area) over again, following the dashed red line.

6.
Fold the underneath layer of paper, aligning edges E and D. Mark the fold, then unfold. This is crease F, which will act as a guide subsequently.

7.
Fold the bottom left-hand corner (1) up to the edge of line D along the dashed red line.

8.
Repeat the previous step with the bottom right-hand corner (2), folding along the dashed red line.

9.
Fold the left-hand side of the napkin inwards at the edge of corner 1, following the dashed red line. Mark the fold, then unfold.

10.
Repeat with the right-hand side. Fold inwards, at the edge of corner 2, following the dashed red line. Mark the fold, then unfold.

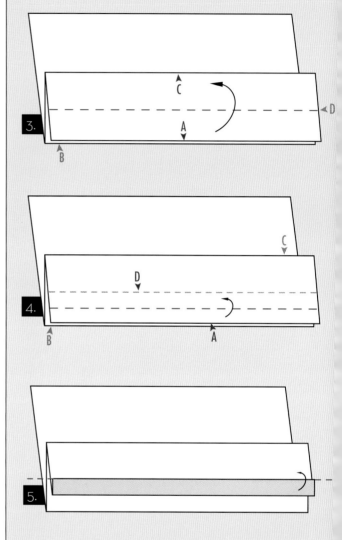
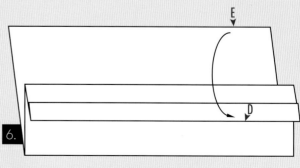

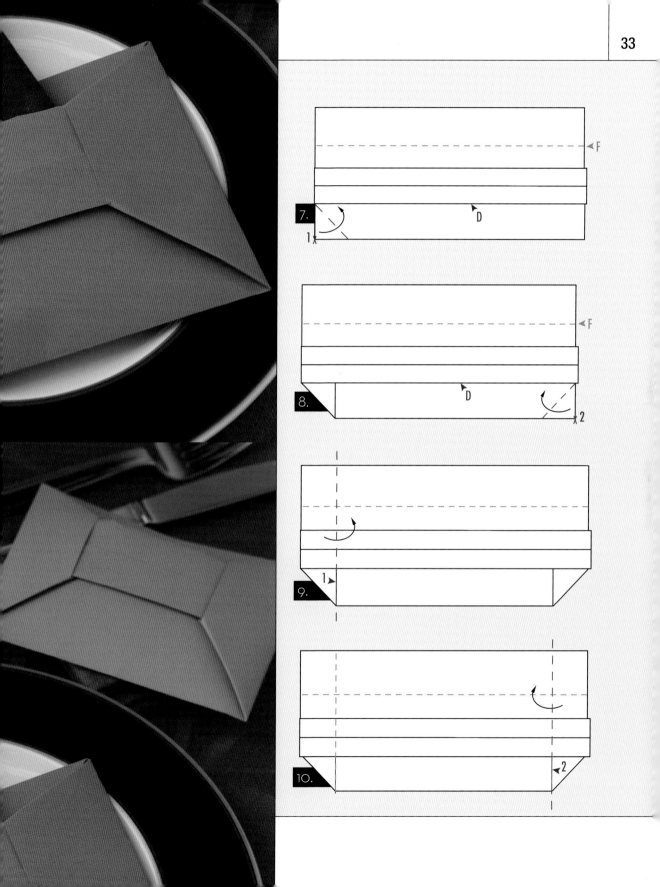

11.

Fold in the left-hand edge of the envelope (bottom layer of paper), following the dashed red line between points G and H. Mark the crease, then unfold.

12.

Repeat the previous step with the right-hand edge of the envelope (bottom layer of paper) along the dashed red line between points I and J. Mark the crease, then unfold.

13.

Fold the central part of the envelope (shaded area) upwards along fold C (red dashed line).

14.

Unfold the bottom left-hand corner. Push corner 1 between the two layers of paper; it will fold out naturally along the creases you made previously to form a triangle.

15.

Unfold the bottom right-hand corner. Push corner 2 between the two layers of paper.

16.

Fold the central section (shaded area) downwards along the dashed red line (crease C).

17.

Open out corner 1, then fold the left-hand side of the envelope (shaded area) inwards along the dashed red line.

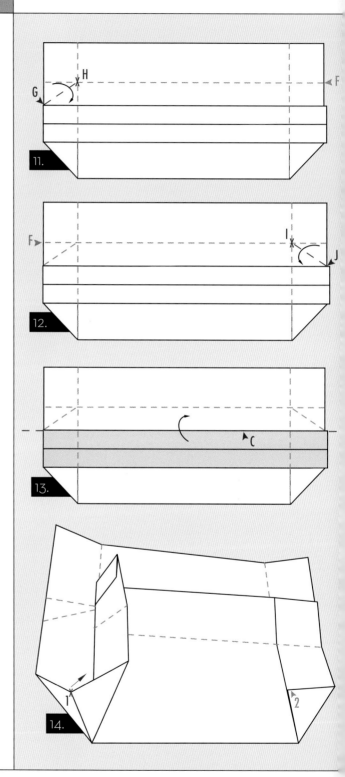

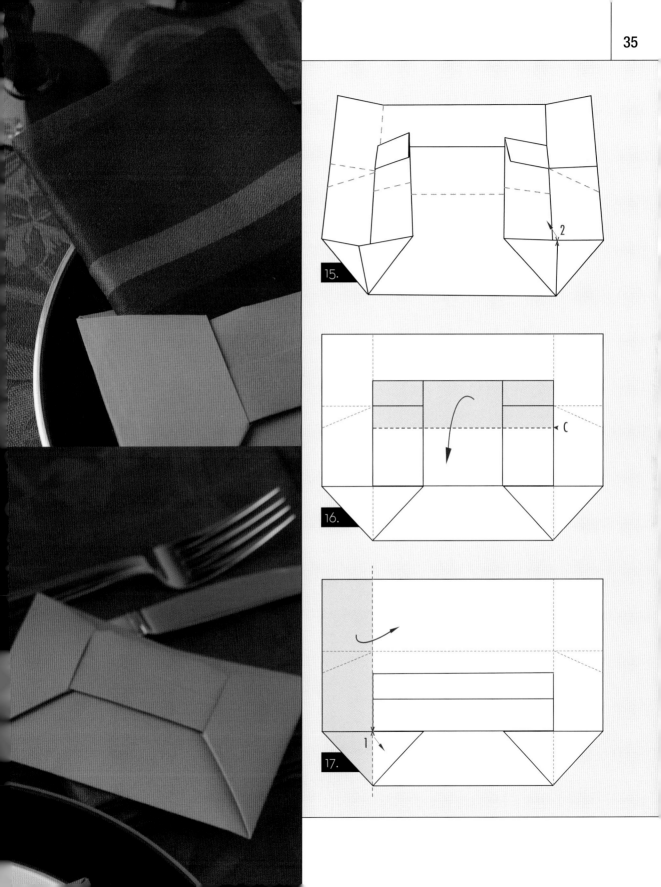

15.

16. C

17. 1

18.

Fold corner 1 along the dashed red line and tuck it under the flap (shaded area).

19.

Open out corner 2, then fold the right-hand side of the envelope (shaded area) inwards, along the dashed red line.

20.

Fold corner 2 along the dashed red line and tuck it under the flap (shaded area).

21.

Fold the top left-hand corner (3) downwards, aligning the edge with crease F and folding along the dashed red line.
Mark the fold, then unfold again.

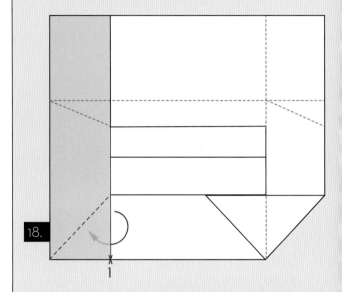

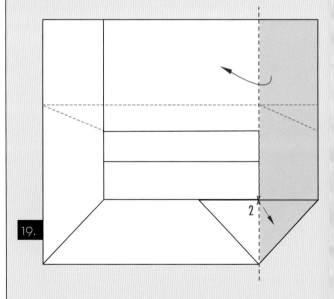

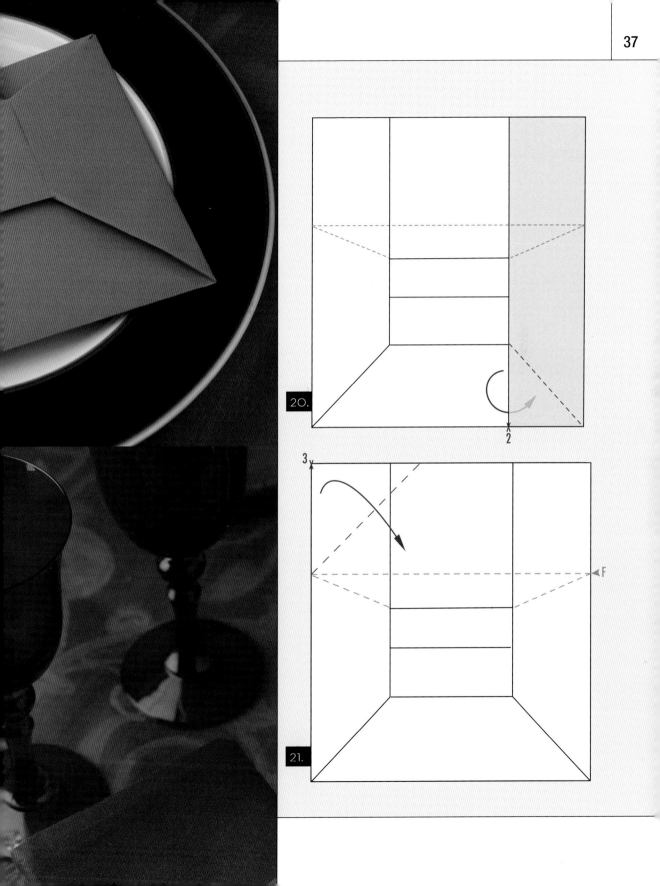

22.
Fold the top right-hand corner (4) downwards, aligning the edge with crease F and folding along the dashed red line.
Mark the fold, then unfold again.

23.
Pinch corner 5 between your fingers (top layer of paper). Tuck it inside the envelope.
Because of the creases you made earlier, the rest of the sheet will sit in place naturally.

24.
Repeat the procedure with corner 6, pinching it between your fingers (top layer of paper) and tucking it inside the envelope.

25.
Tuck the shaded part inside the envelope, folding along the dashed red line.
Slip the napkin into the envelope.

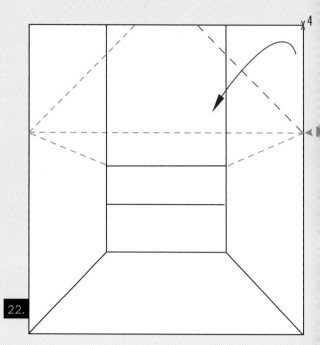

22.

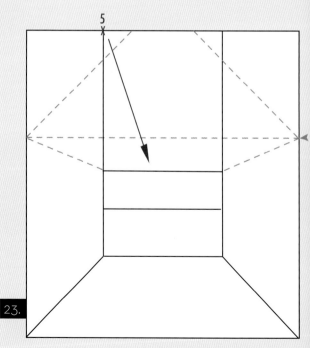

23.

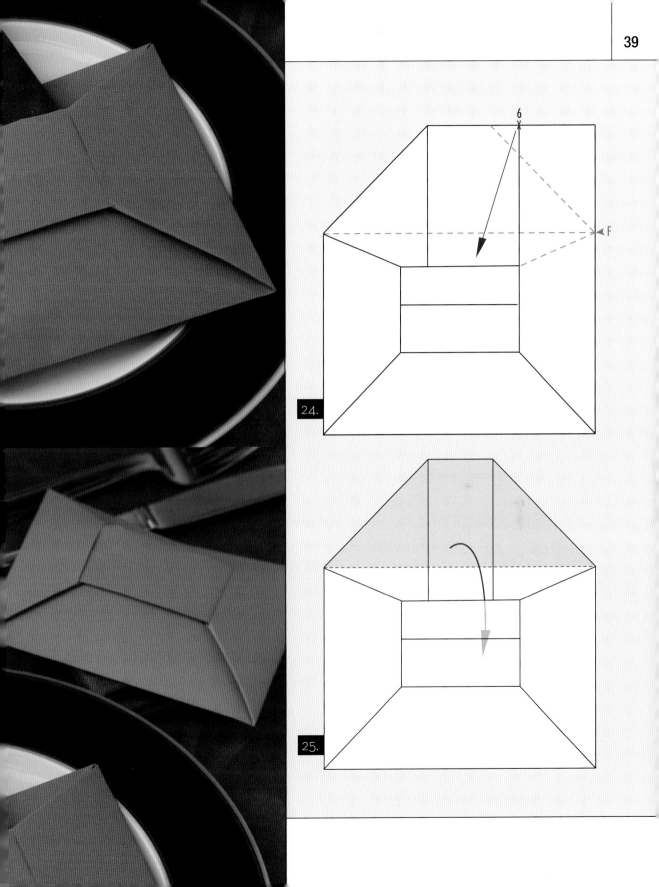

24.

25.

Evening wear

1.

Lay a square napkin on the work surface, wrong side up. Fold in half vertically, following the dashed red line. Iron to mark the fold. Unfold. Fold in half horizontally, following the dashed blue line. Iron and then unfold.
You will use these creases as guides later.

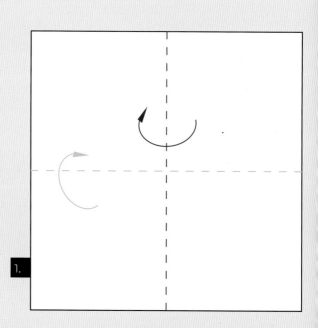

1.

2.
Fold two opposite corners to the centre of the napkin so that points B and D meet at point E, following the dashed red lines. Iron the folds.

3.
Fold the other two corners to the centre of the napkin along the dashed red lines so that points A and C meet at point E.
Iron the folds.

4.
Rotate the napkin, then fold it in half horizontally along the dashed red line. Iron.

5.
Pleat the centre of the rectangle to form the bow.

6.
Wrap a piece of ribbon round the centre of the bow. Staple it together on the underside.

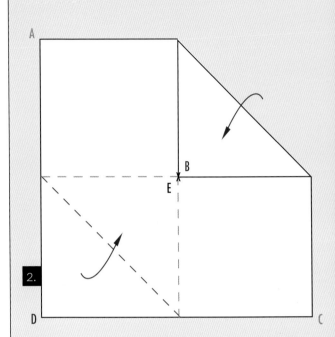

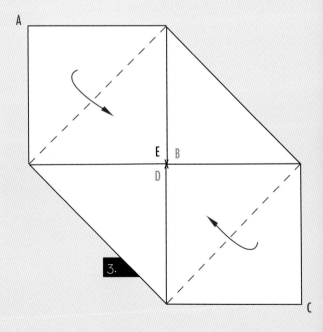

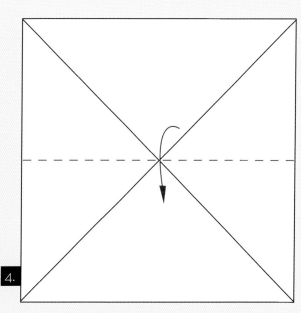

4.

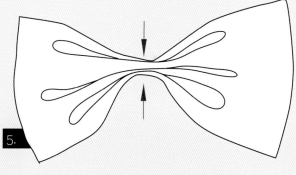

5.

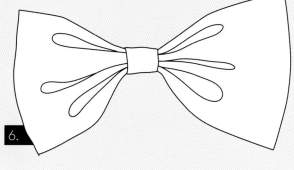

6.

Lipstick

1.

Lay a square napkin on the work surface, wrong side up. Fold in half diagonally.

2.

Rotate the napkin so the top of the triangle (B) points upwards. Fold the right- and left-hand corners (C and A) up to point B. Align A/B and C/B, following the dashed red lines.

3.

Fold the bottom third of the diamond upwards. Fold along the dashed red line. Spray with starch and iron to press the folds.

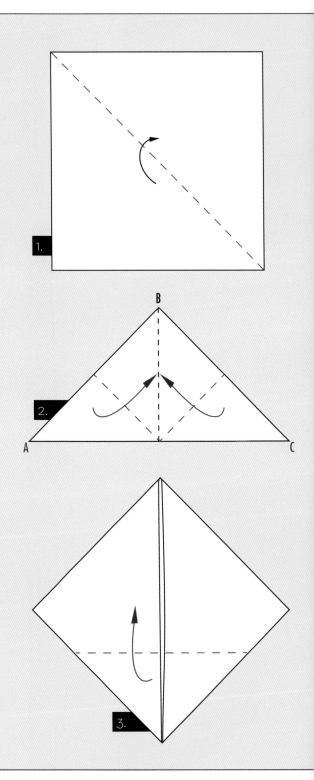

4.
Fold the point of this flap downwards to the bottom edge of the napkin.

5.
Iron, then flip the napkin over.

6.
Fold the right-hand third of the napkin to the centre following the dashed red line.

7.
Fold the point of this flap under again. Iron.

8.
Fold the left-hand point of the napkin inwards along the dashed red line. Iron to mark the fold.

9.
Following the dashed red line, fold the left-hand edge of the napkin to the right. Slip the bottom left-hand corner (A) inside the right-hand flap (B). This should ensure that the napkin does not unfold.

10.
Flip the napkin over. Slip your hand inside to push it into shape.

11.
Gently peel down the two outer layers of the napkin (1 and 2).
Tuck them into the base.

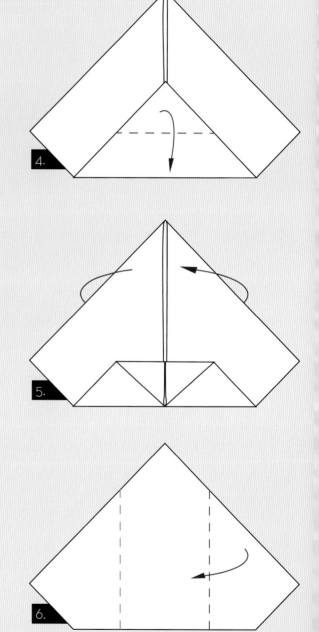

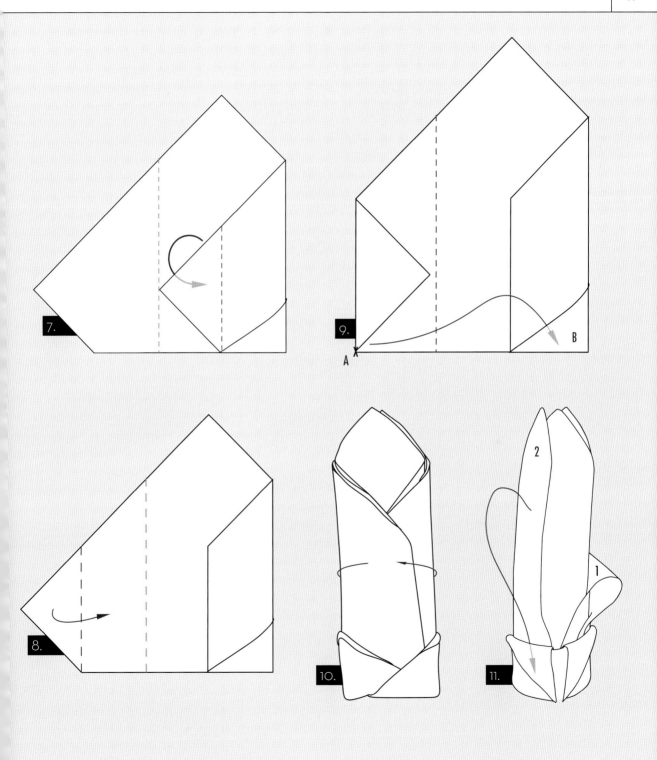

So
glamorous

Square fold

1.
This works better with a small napkin (28 x 28cm/11 x 11in) or a thin napkin folded into four. Lay a square napkin on the work surface, wrong side up. Fold in half vertically, following the dashed red line. Iron to mark the fold. Unfold. Fold in half horizontally, following the dashed blue line. Iron and then unfold. These creases will act as guides later.

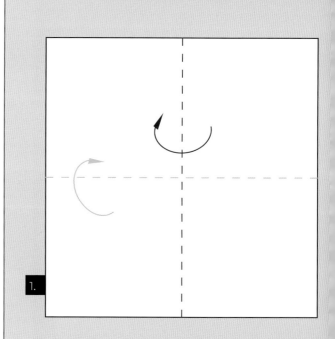

1.

2.

Fold two opposite corners to the centre of the napkin along the dashed red lines, so that points B and D meet at point E. Iron the folds.

3.

Fold the other two corners to the centre of the napkin along the dashed red lines so that points A and C meet at point E. Iron the folds.

4.

Rotate the napkin (the edges must be parallel). Fold the point of one triangle outwards along the dashed red line. The fold line should be approximately 2cm (1in) from the edge. Spray with starch and iron to press the folds.

5.

Repeat the previous step with the other three points. Spray with starch and iron to press the folds.

6.

Flip the napkin over.

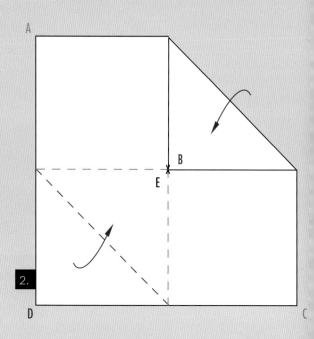

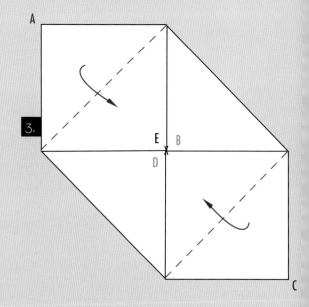

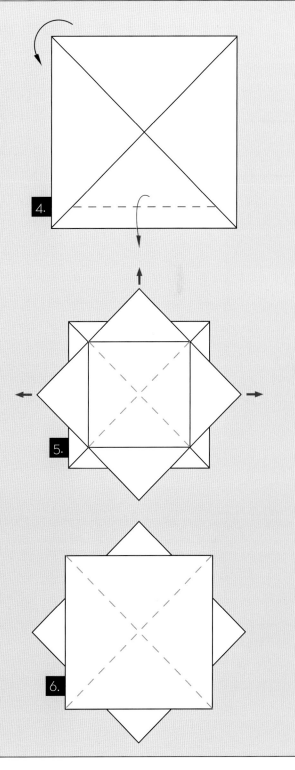

4.

5.

6.

An elegant twist

1.

Lay a square napkin on the work surface, wrong side up. Fold in half horizontally following the dashed red line. Make sure that the open edge is towards you. Spray with starch. Iron to press the fold.

2.

Fold in half vertically, following the dashed red line. Iron to mark the fold, then unfold the napkin. This crease will act as a guide.

3.

Starting at point A, roll up the left-hand side of the napkin until the bottom left-hand corner (B) is aligned with the bottom right-hand corner (C).

4.

Rotate the napkin. Fold point B/C up behind the napkin, following the dashed red line.

5.

Slip your hand inside the cone and push it into shape.

55

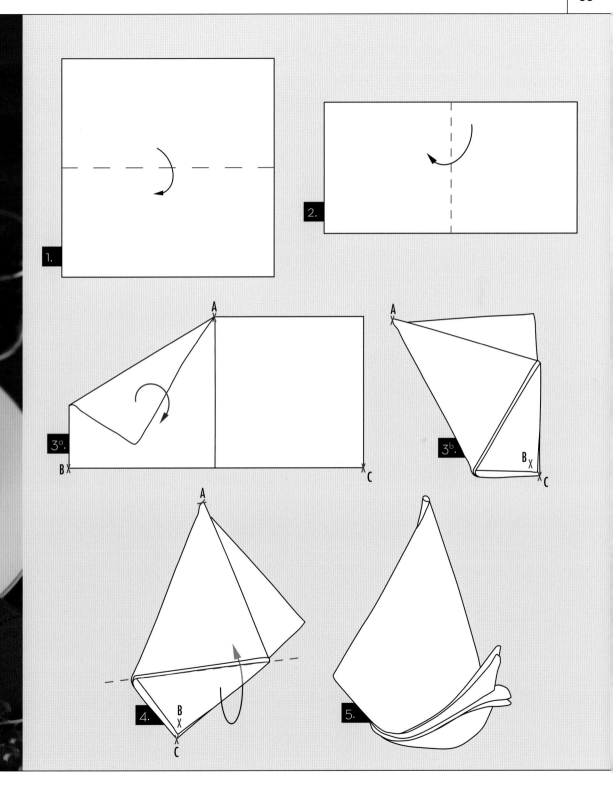

Small talk

1.

Lay a square napkin on the work surface, wrong side up. Fold the bottom third of the napkin up to the centre along dashed red line C, aligning edge D with dashed grey line B. Iron the fold.

2.

Fold the top third of the napkin down. Align edge A with edge C; iron the fold.

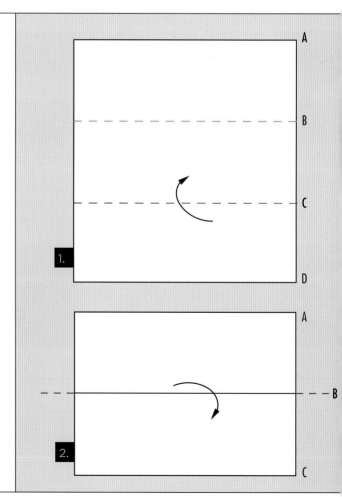

3.

Fold the left half of the napkin down, forming a right angle. Fold along the dashed red line, starting at the central point (A).

4.

Fold the right half of the napkin in the same way, following the dashed red line. Iron, then flip the napkin over.

5.

Roll up the right-hand part of the napkin as far as the base of the triangle.

6.

Repeat this step on the left-hand side. When both rolls have been formed, flip the napkin over.

7.

Fold the bottom right-hand corner (2) towards the top corner of the triangle (1), bringing point 2 to point 1 by folding along the dashed red line.

8.

Repeat the previous step with the bottom left-hand corner (3), bringing point 3 to point 1 by folding along the dashed red line.

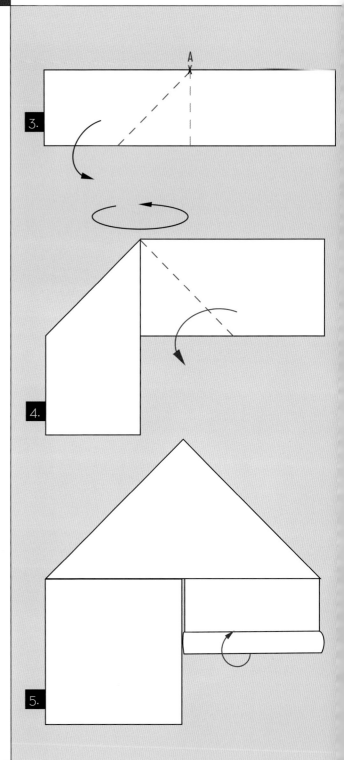

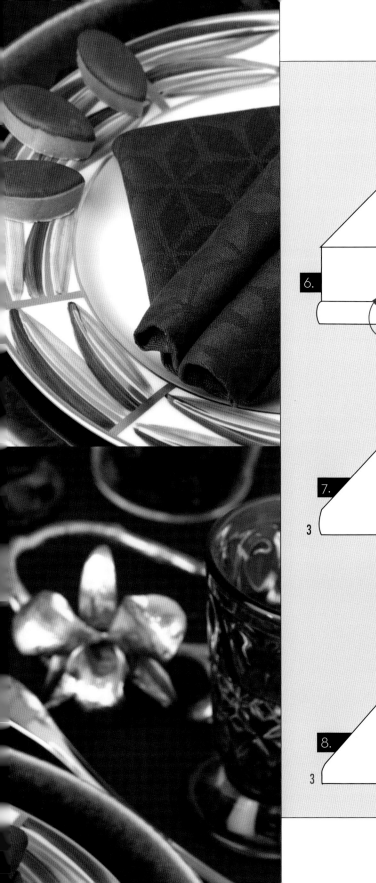

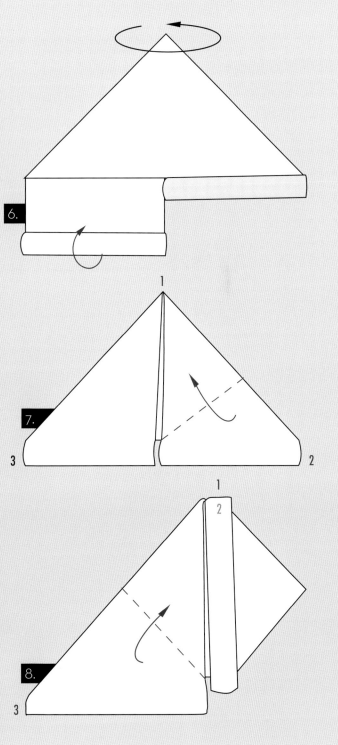

6.

7.

8.

Minimalist

1.

Lay a square napkin on the work surface, wrong side up. Fold in half diagonally.

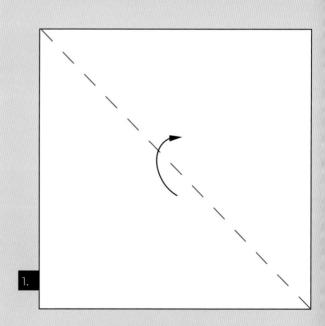

1.

2.
Rotate the napkin so the top of the triangle (B) points upwards. Fold the right- and left-hand corners (A and C) to the top point of the triangle (B), following the dashed red lines.

3.
Spray lightly with starch. Iron to mark the folds, then flip the napkin over.

4.
Fold the napkin in half horizontally, following the dashed red line and bringing point D to point B.

5.
Bring corners E and C together at the back of the napkin. The opening edge B/D/F should remain facing you.

6.
Place the napkin on the base of the triangle (the longest side).

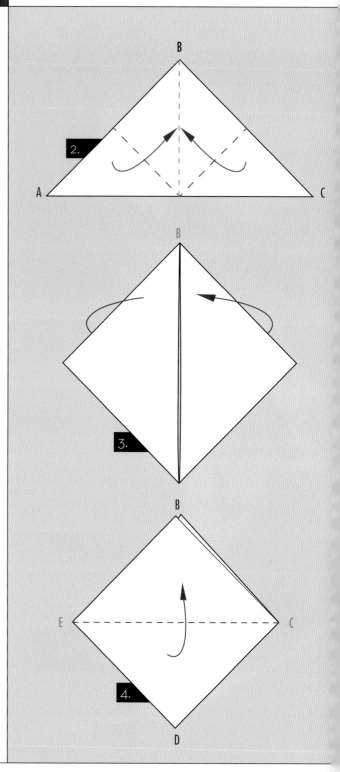

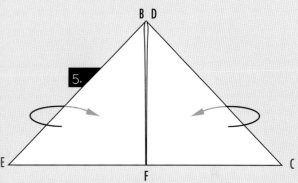

5.

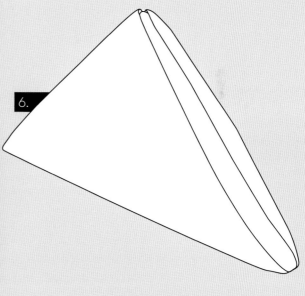

6.

Pretty in pleats

1.

Lay a square napkin on the work surface, wrong side up. Fold in half horizontally along the dashed red line. Spray with starch and iron to press the fold.

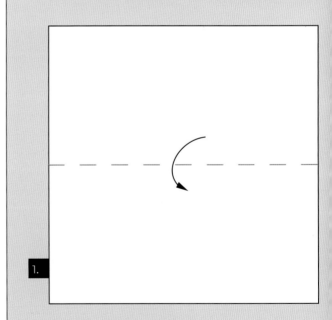

1.

2.

Place your finger on point A (middle of the top edge of the napkin). Pinch corner B (top layer of the napkin) – a diagonal forms between points A and B. Rotate this line, bringing corner B to corner C. This will form a triangle.

3.

Take the right-hand point of this triangle (B) and fold it to the left-hand corner (D) along the dashed red line.

4.

Place your finger on point A. Pinch corner C (top layer of the napkin) – a diagonal forms between points A and C. Rotate this line, aligning corner C and corner B. This will form a triangle.

5.

Take the right-hand point of this triangle (D) and fold it to the left-hand corner along the dashed red line.

6.

Stand the fan up. Shape each pleat to ensure your napkin is well turned out.

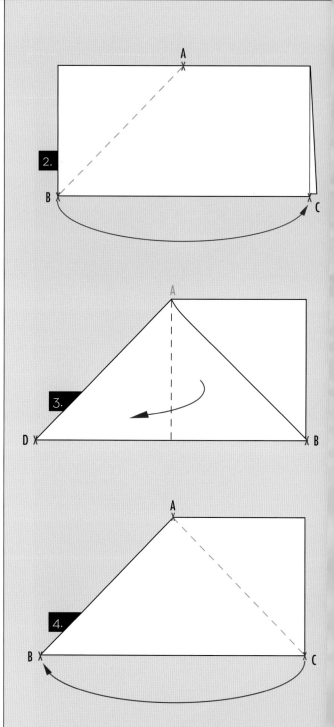

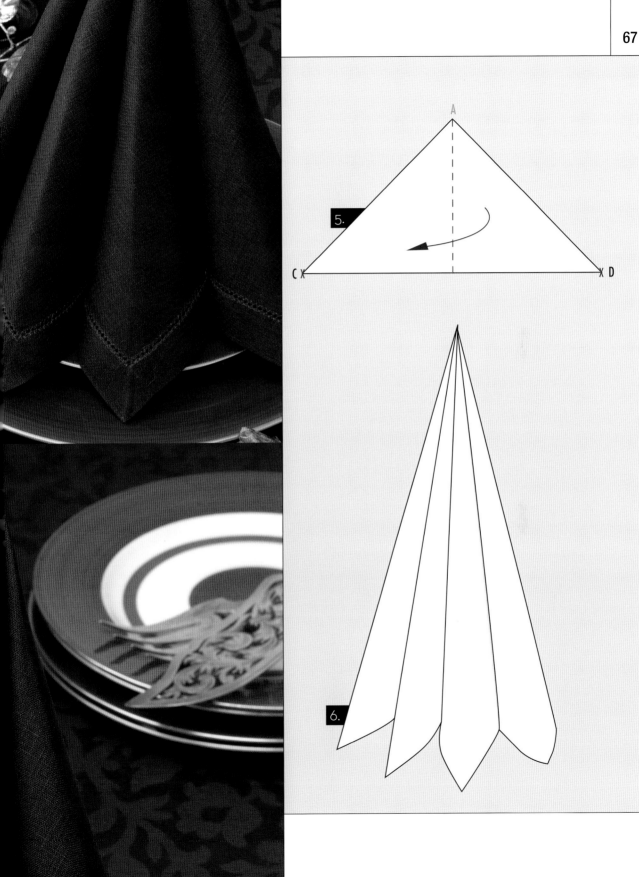

Rising star

1.

Lay a square napkin on the work surface, wrong side up. Fold in half horizontally following the dashed red line. Spray with starch. Iron to mark the crease, then unfold the napkin.

2.

Fold the bottom of the napkin up to the centre along the dashed red line, aligning edge A with the central crease. Iron to mark the fold.

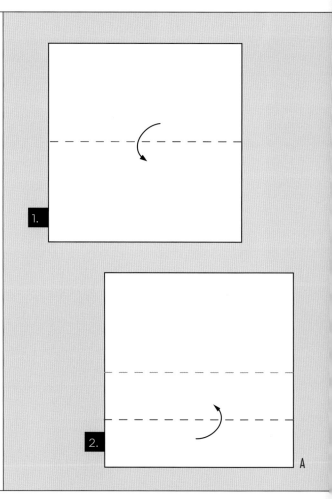

3.
Repeat this step with the top of the napkin, folding along the dashed red line and aligning edge B with the central crease. Iron to mark the fold.

4.
Fold the napkin in half horizontally along the dashed red line. Iron to press the fold.

5.
Fold in half vertically, following the dashed red line. Iron to mark the fold, then unfold again.

6.
Fold the right of the napkin towards the centre along the dashed red line, aligning edge A with the central crease. Iron to press the fold.

7.
Fold the left of the napkin towards the centre along the dashed red line, aligning edge B with the central crease. Flip the napkin over.

8.
Once you have flipped the napkin over, fold it in half vertically along the dashed red line. Iron to press the fold.

9.
Stand the napkin facing you as shown in the diagram. Prop it on the bottom back corners.

10.
Take hold of corner A (shaded area) and pull it gently downwards.

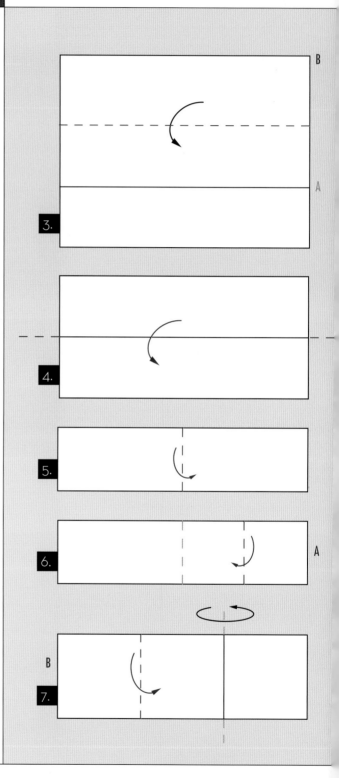

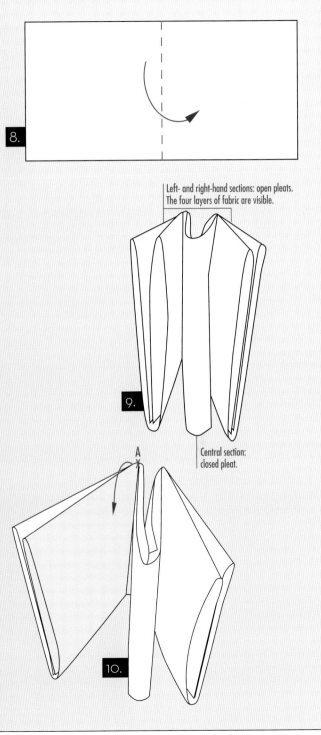

8.

Left- and right-hand sections: open pleats.
The four layers of fabric are visible.

9.

Central section:
closed pleat.

A

10.

11.

Repeat the previous step with internal right-hand corner (2), taking hold of corner B and pulling it gently downwards.

12.

a) Fold the right-hand side of the napkin, bringing point 1 to point 2.
b) Once folded, the right-hand side should resemble the diagram.

13.

Do the same with the left-hand side, bringing point 3 to point 4.

14.

Fold the left-hand part of the napkin (shaded area) down towards the work surface.

15.

Likewise fold the right-hand part of the napkin (shaded area) down towards the work surface.

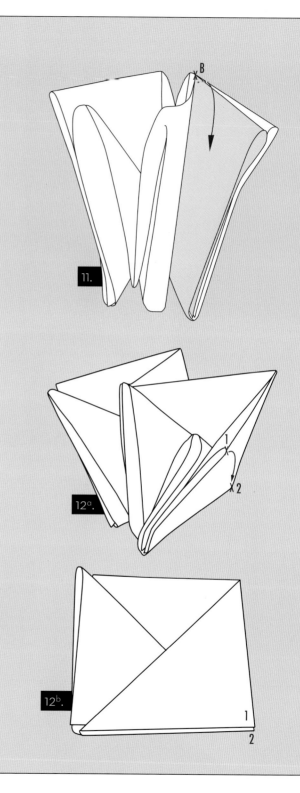

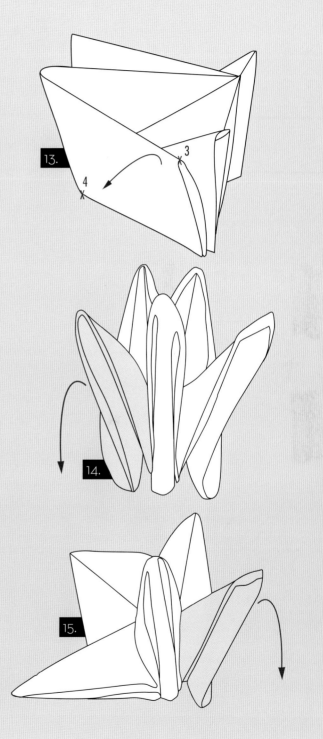

Love
hearts

Pretty heart

1.

Lay a square napkin on the work surface, wrong side up. Fold in half horizontally following the dashed red line. Spray with a little starch and iron to press the fold.

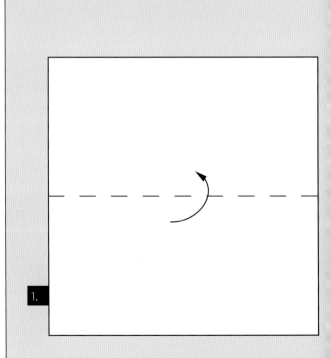

2.

Fold this rectangle in half horizontally, folding the top half of the napkin downwards along the dashed red line. Iron.

3.

Fold the right-hand half of the napkin upwards along the dashed red line, starting at the central point (A) and forming a right angle.

4.

Fold the left-hand half of the napkin upwards along the dashed red line. Iron, then flip the napkin over, point downwards.

5.

Fold the left-hand corner of the napkin (A) along the dashed red line. Iron to press the fold.

6.

Repeat the previous step with the other three corners (B, C and D). Iron, then flip the napkin over.

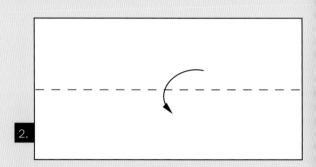

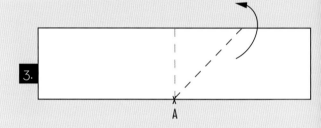

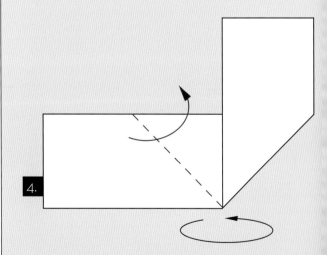

A

5.

B C   D

6.

Hearts uplifted!

1.

Lay a square napkin on the work surface, wrong side up. A thin or non-woven napkin is better for this project. Fold the top quarter (A) and the bottom quarter (b) to the centre of the napkin (C) along the dashed red lines. Spray with starch and iron to press the folds.

2.

Fold the napkin in half horizontally along the dashed red line, aligning edges 1 and 2. Spray, then iron to press the fold.

3.

Fold in half vertically along the dashed red line. Iron to mark the central fold. Unfold.

4.

Form a heart by bringing the two ends of the napkin together. Place the napkin on one edge.

Note: Spraying fabric napkins with starch at each stage will ensure they hold their shape better.

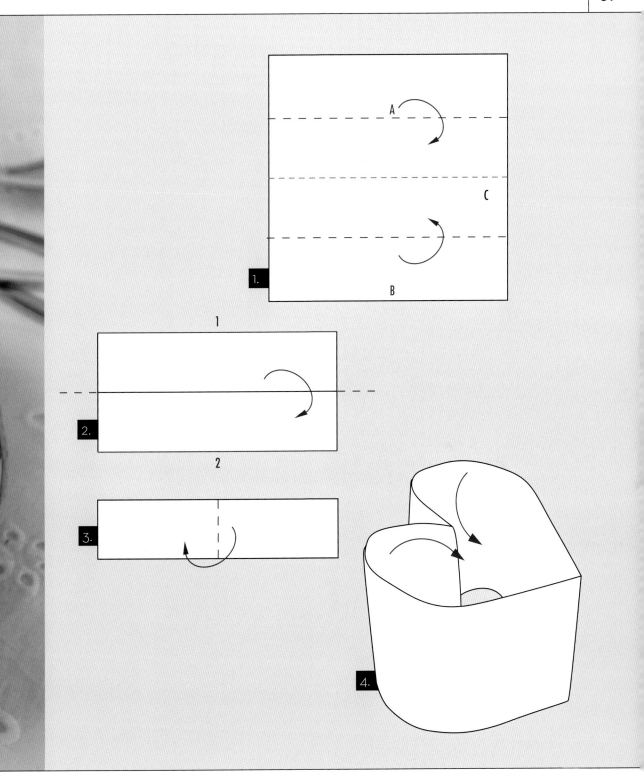

Heart strings

1.

Lay a square napkin on the work surface, wrong side up. Fold in half diagonally along the dashed red line. Iron to press the fold.

2.

Rotate the napkin so the top of the triangle points upwards. Roll the napkin up starting from the longest side. Hold the rolled-up napkin by both ends. Twist it (as if you were wringing water out of the fabric).

3.

Without letting go of the ends, bend the twisted napkin in the middle and form the heart shape. Knot a ribbon around the ends to hold them in place.

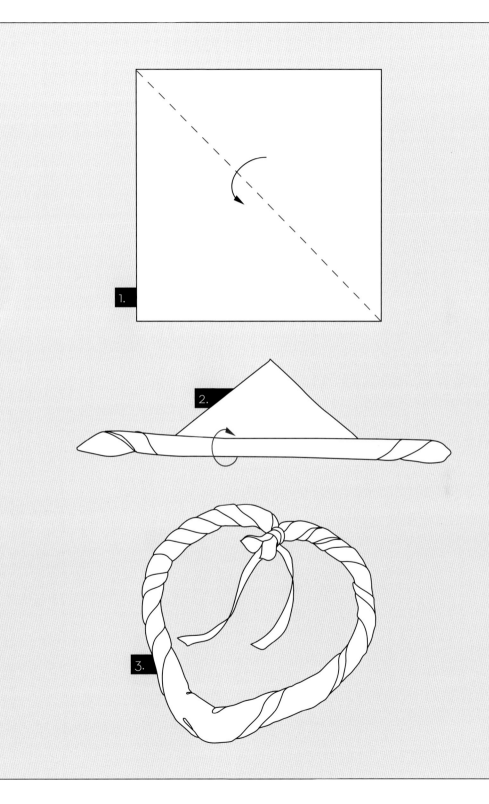

A good heart

1.

Lay a square napkin on the work surface, wrong side up. Fold the top quarter (A) and the bottom quarter (B) to the centre of the napkin (C) along the dashed red lines. Spray with starch and iron to press the folds.

2.

Fold the right-hand and left-hand quarters of the napkin inwards, bringing A to B and C to B by folding along the dashed red lines.

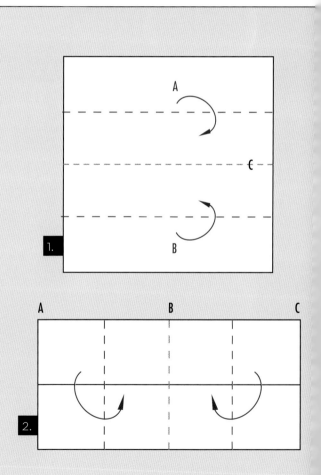

3.

Fold the napkin in half one more time, right-hand side over left-hand side. Iron.

4.

Use a hobby knife to cut two strips from a sheet of translucent plastic film: one 30cm x 2cm (12 x 1in), the other 25cm x 2cm (10 x 1in). Fold each strip in half in the middle. Tuck the fold in the smaller strip into the fold in the bigger strip. Pinch the base and staple.

5.

Holding the two left-hand strips between your thumb and forefinger, align the ends. Do the same with the right-hand strips.

6.

Form the heart shape. Bend the strips inwards, bringing your thumbs together. Check that the ends of the four bands are all aligned. Staple. Place the heart on the napkin.

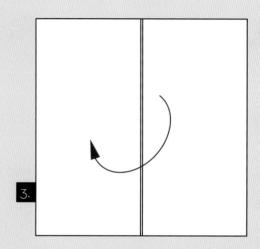

3.

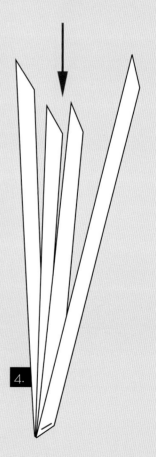

4.

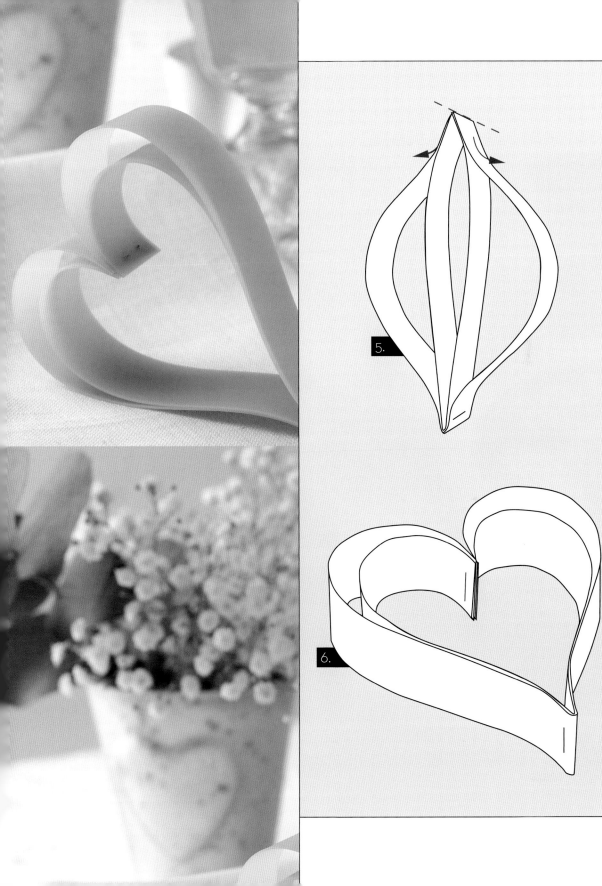

5.

6.

Oriental
style

Fan

1.

Lay a square napkin on the work surface, wrong side up. Fold in half horizontally along the dashed red line (a). Iron to mark the fold. Fold in half horizontally again along the dashed blue line (b). Iron to mark the fold. Unfold the napkin completely.

2.

Make accordion pleats. Alternate valley folds (dashed red lines) with mountain folds (dashed blue lines). Form regular pleats. The creases you made in stage 1 (dashed grey lines) will help you with this. Iron to press the folds.

3.

When you reach the end of the accordion pleats, fold the napkin into two equal halves.

4.

Slip a napkin ring over the base of the fan, or knot a tie around it to hold it in place.

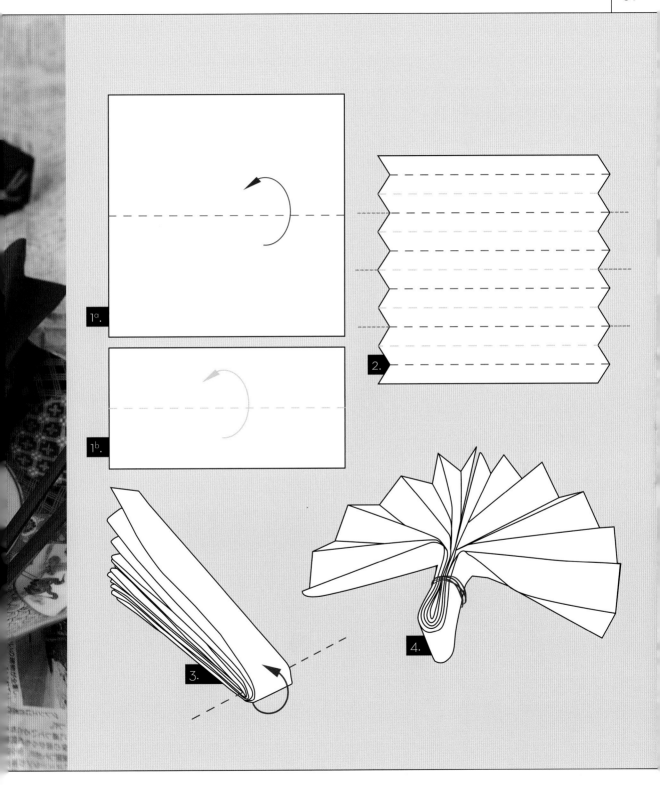

Chopsticks

1.

Lay a square napkin on the work surface, right side up. Fold in half horizontally (dashed red line). Iron to mark the fold. Unfold the napkin. Fold in half vertically (dashed blue line). Iron to mark the fold. Unfold the napkin.

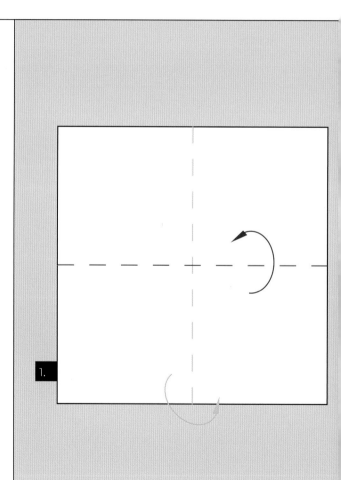

2.
Fold the left side (A) and right side (B) of the napkin to the centre along the dashed red lines. Spray with starch and iron to press the folds.

3.
Open out the internal corners (1, 2, 3, 4) along the dashed red lines. Spray with starch, then iron to press the folds. Rotate the napkin 90°.

4.
Lay the chopsticks on the right- and left-hand sides of the napkin. Roll each side towards the centre. (This can also be done without a baguette inside; it will still hold its shape.)

5.
Wind a tie around the middle to keep it together and knot it underneath.

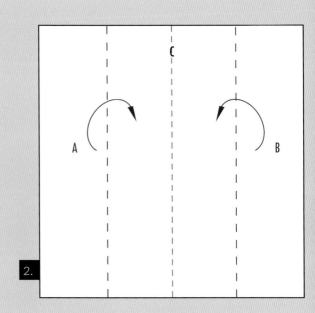

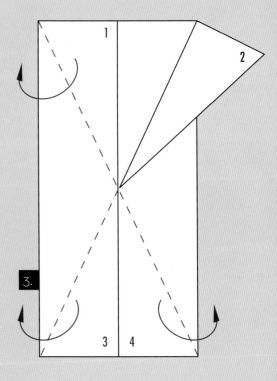

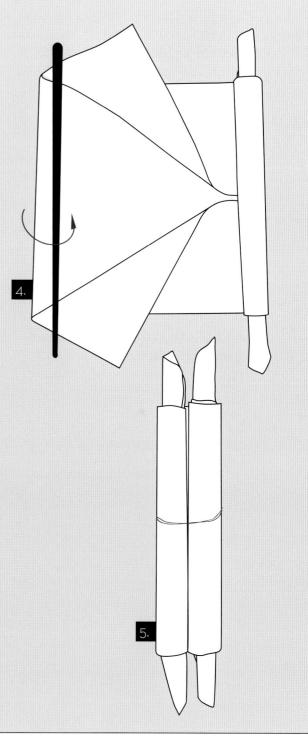

4.

5.

Kimono

1.

Lay a square napkin on the work surface, wrong side up. Fold in half vertically along the dashed red line. Iron to mark the fold. Unfold again. Fold the napkin in half horizontally along the dashed blue line. Iron to mark the fold. Unfold again. These creases will serve as guides subsequently.

2.

Fold the left side of the napkin towards the centre along the dashed red line, aligning edge 2 with the central crease (1). Iron to mark the fold.

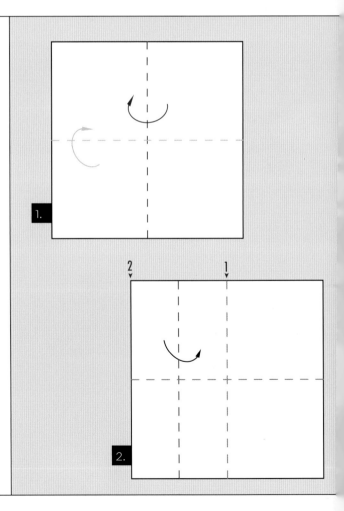

3.
Fold the right side of the napkin towards the centre along the dashed red line, aligning edge 3 with the central crease (1). Iron to mark the fold.

4.
Unfold the whole napkin. Make a new fold by aligning fold 4 with the central crease (1), following the dashed red line. Iron and then unfold.

5.
Make another fold on the right-hand side of the napkin. Align fold 5 with the central crease, following the dashed red line. Iron and then unfold.

6.
Fold the strip of fabric between creases 7 and 5 under the central part (shaded area between folds 6 and 7). Iron to press the fold.

7.
Fold the strip of fabric between creases 4 and 6 under the central part (shaded area between folds 6 and 7). Iron to press the fold.

8.
Fold the napkin in half horizontally backwards along the dashed red line. Iron to press the fold.

9.
Fold the right-hand corner (A) along the dashed red line, aligning the edge of the napkin and the right-hand edge of the central band. Iron to mark the fold, then unfold.

10.
Fold the left-hand corner (B) along the dashed red line, aligning the edge of the napkin and the left-hand edge of the central band. Iron to mark the fold, then unfold.

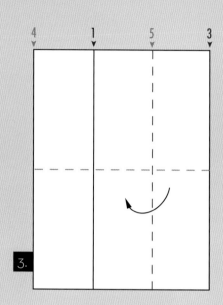

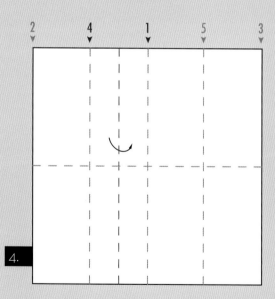

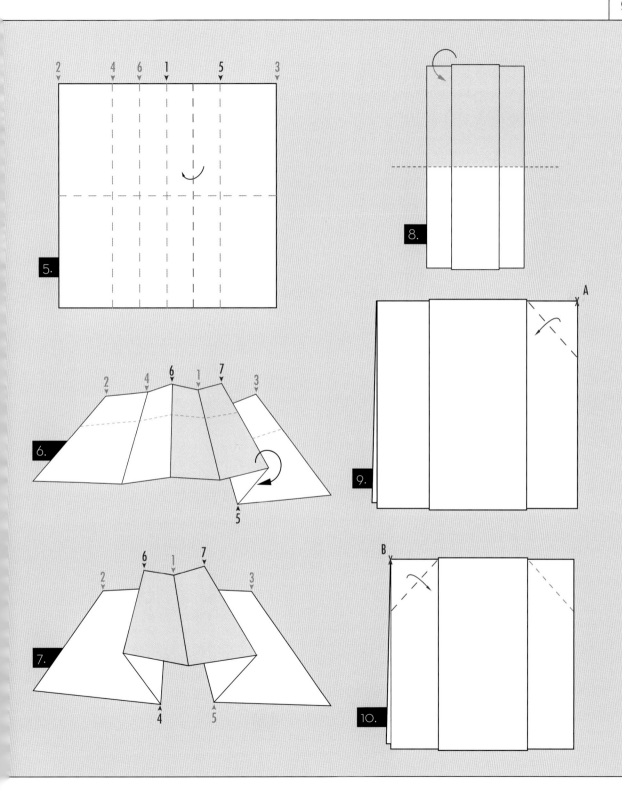

11.
Fold the first layer of the napkin (shaded area) over the central section. Corner A will open naturally into a triangle.

12.
Repeat on the left-hand side. Fold the first layer of the napkin (shaded area) over the central section. Corner B will open naturally into a triangle.

13.
Iron the folds, then flip over.

14.
Fold the top layer of the napkin upwards along the dashed red line. Iron.

15.
Pull the shaded sections gently downwards to form the sleeves of the kimono.

16.
Give the napkin a final iron.

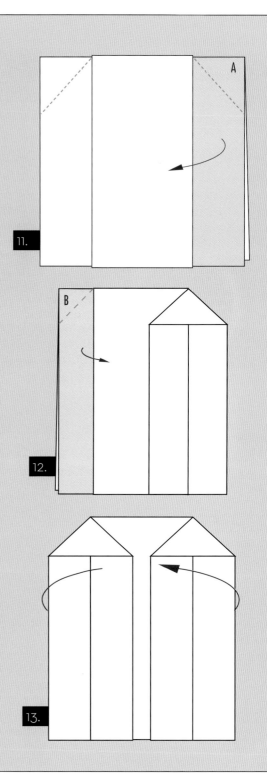

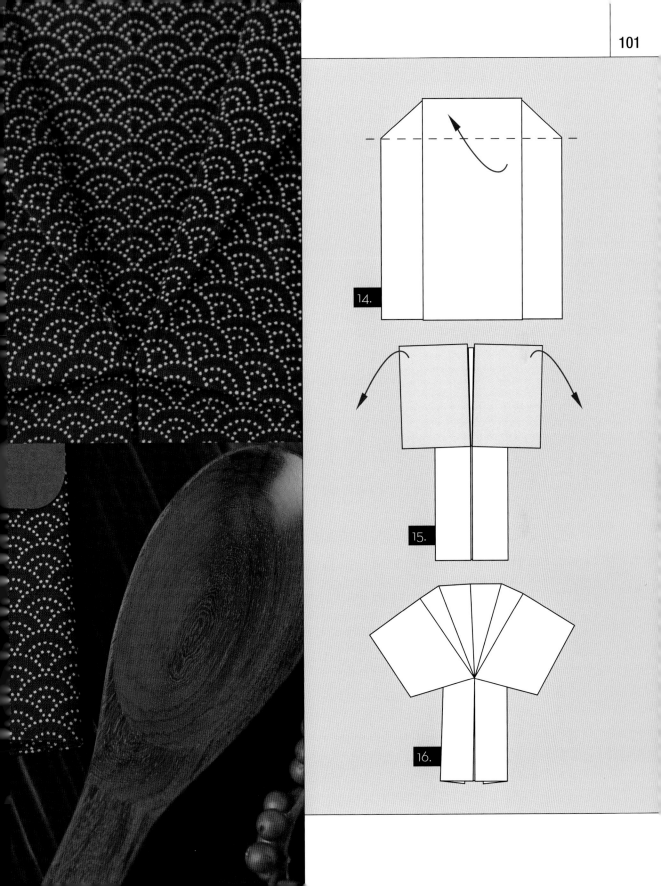

14.

15.

16.

Sash style

1.

Lay a square napkin on the work surface, wrong side up. Fold the top quarter (A) and the bottom quarter (B) to the centre of the napkin (C) along the dashed red lines. Spray with starch and iron to press the folds.

2.

Fold the left-hand quarter (1) and the right-hand quarter (2) to the centre of the napkin (C) along the dashed red lines. Iron to press the fold.

3.

Fold the right-and left-hand thirds of the napkin inwards along the dashed red lines. Iron.

4.

Cut out a fabric rectangle measuring approximately 25 x 15cm (10 x 6in) (match the dimensions to the size of the napkin to be decorated). To give a clean finish to the edges, form a 'hem' by turning in a few centimetres of fabric all round the edges. Iron to press the folds. Wrap this strip of fabric around the napkin.

5.

Use two lengths of ribbon, twine or cord approximately 25cm (10in) in length to make a single tie. As shown in the diagram, tie them into a reef knot. Centre this knot on the front of the napkin. Knot the tie behind.

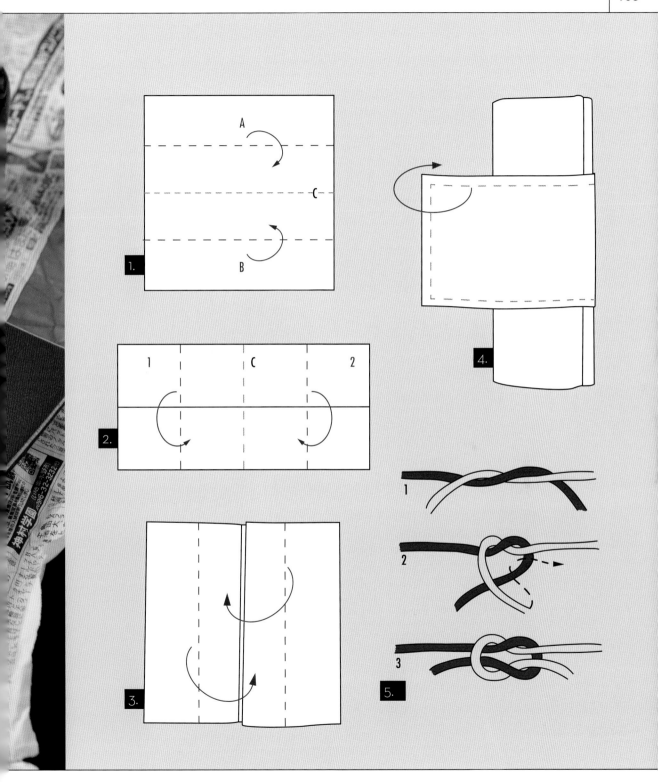

Furoshiki

1.
Lay a square napkin on the work surface, wrong side up. Place the object to be wrapped in the centre. Spherical items such as bread rolls work best.

2.
Knot together corners A and B of the napkin.

3.
Knot together corners C and D of the napkin.

4.
Pass the right-hand handle (C/D) under the left-hand handle (A/B).

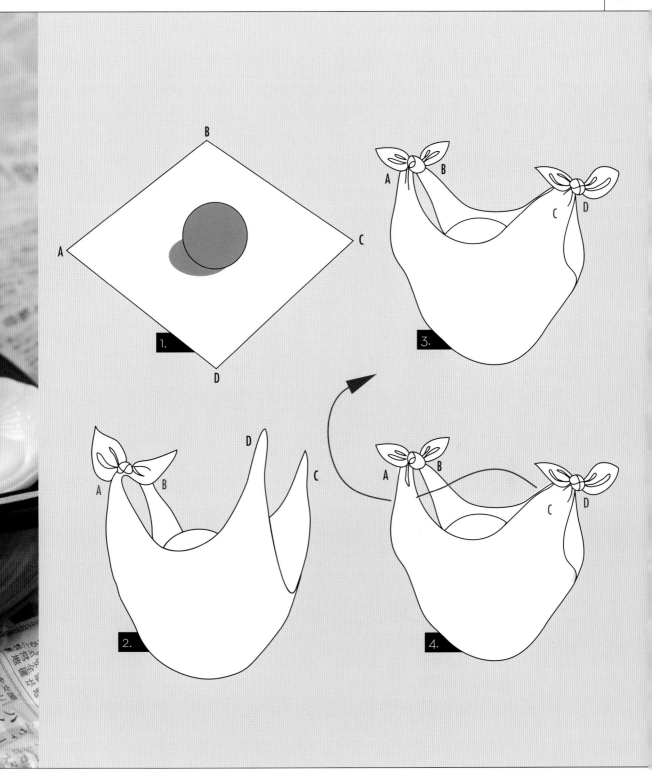

In the garden

Lotus flower

1.

Lay a square napkin on the work surface, wrong side up. Fold in half diagonally. Iron to mark the fold. Unfold. Repeat on the other diagonal. Iron and then unfold.

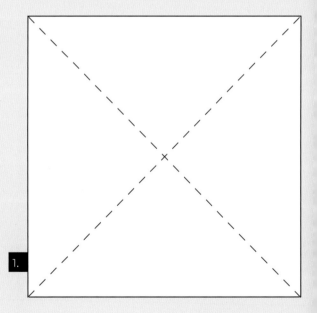

1.

2.

Fold each corner of the napkin into the centre along the dashed red lines, so that points A, B, C and D meet at point E. Iron the folds.

3.

Repeat the previous step. Fold each corner of the napkin into the centre along the dashed red lines again, so that points F, G, H and I meet at point E. Iron the folds. Flip the napkin over.

4.

Having flipped the napkin, fold the corners to the centre a final time along the dashed red lines. Iron the folds.

5.

Place your finger in the centre of the napkin to hold the four flaps in place. One by one, take hold of one of the tabs underneath each corner and pull them gently outwards and upwards.

6.

Keeping your finger pressed in the centre of the napkin to stop it from unfolding, pull the tabs underneath the flower between each petal gently outwards.

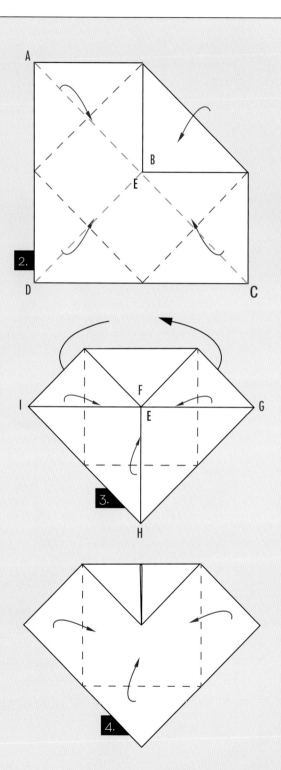

111

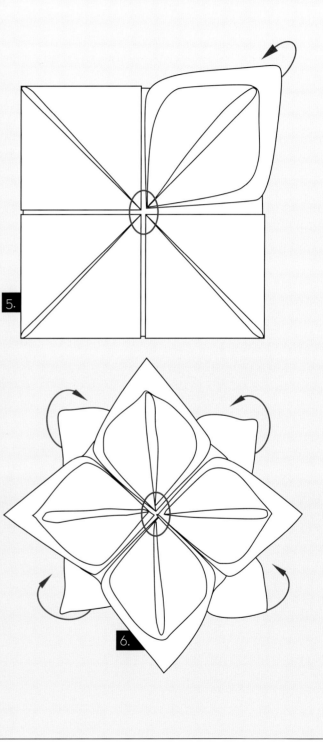

5.

6.

Tulip

1.

Lay a square napkin on the work surface, wrong side up. Fold in half diagonally. Bring point B to point B'.

2.

Rotate the napkin so the top of the triangle (B) points upwards. Fold the right- and left-hand corners (C and A) to the top point of the triangle (B), along the dashed red lines.

3.

Fold the left- and right-hand corners (E and G) to the centre (F), along the dashed red lines. Spray with starch, then iron the folds.

4.

Following the dashed red lines, fold the top points of the napkin (A and C) downwards. Do this with just a single layer of the napkin. Iron to press the folds.

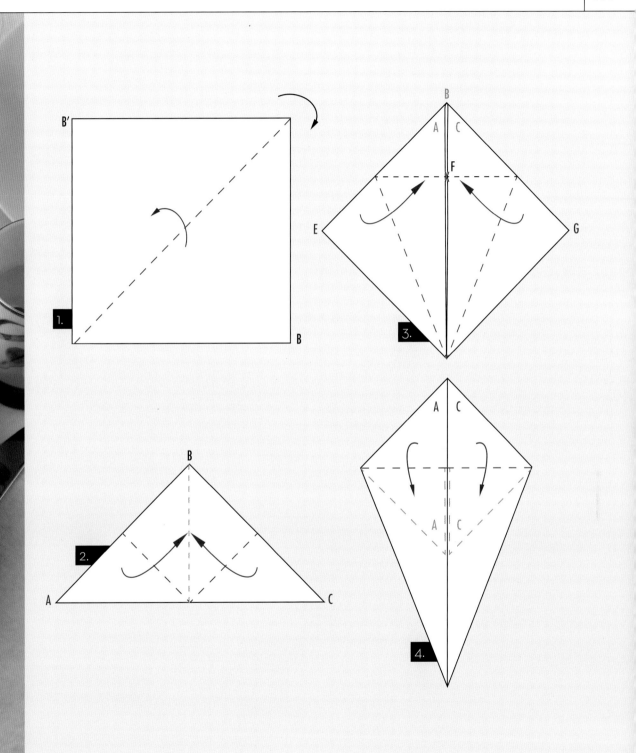

Rosebud

1.
Lay a square napkin on the work surface, wrong side up. Fold in half diagonally.

2.
Rotate the napkin so the top of the triangle points upwards. Roll the napkin up starting from the longest side.

3.
Roll the napkin on itself in a spiral.

4.
Tuck the end of the rolled napkin into the central folds. Flip the napkin over.

5.
Pull the centre of the napkin gently upwards to give it an attractive shape.

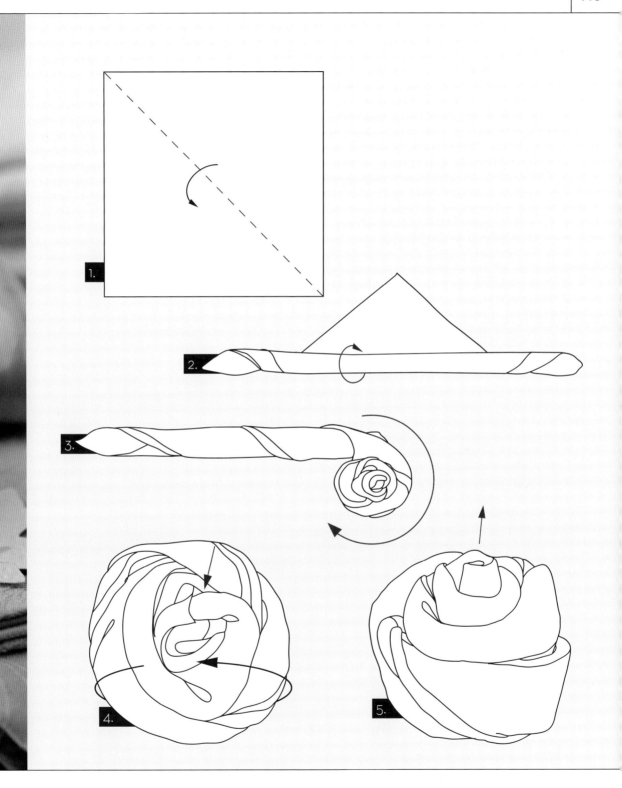

The beating of wings

1.
Lay a square napkin on the work surface, wrong side up. A finer fabric is best for this project. Fold in half vertically along the dashed red line. Iron to press the fold.

2.
Fold the top layer of the napkin in half horizontally, aligning edges A and B.

3.
Fold the top layer of the napkin in half again vertically, aligning edges A and C. Iron to mark the fold. Then open out the napkin along fold B.

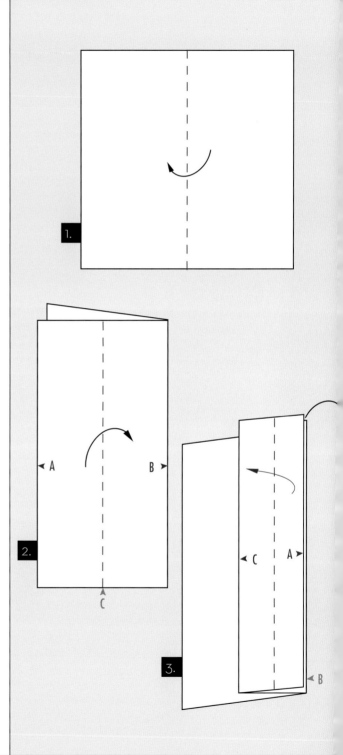

4.

Fold the right-hand edge (C) to the central crease (B). Iron. Unfold all folds. The right-hand side of the napkin is divided into four equal parts.

5.

Fold the right half of the napkin into accordion pleats. Use the creases you made previously as guides. Alternate mountain and valley folds, forming a zigzag of eight equal parts. Iron to press the folds. Flip the napkin over.

6.

Rotate the napkin and place the accordion folds at the top of the rectangle. Fold the napkin in half vertically. Iron to mark the fold, then unfold again.

7.

Fold the top right-hand corner to the bottom of the napkin. Bring point D to point E by folding along the dashed red line. Iron to press the fold.

8.

Fold the top left-hand corner to the bottom of the napkin. Bring point F to point E by folding along the dashed red line. Iron to press the fold, then flip the napkin over.

9.

Fold the bottom right-hand corner to the top of the napkin along the dashed red line, bringing point 2 to point 1. Iron to press the fold.

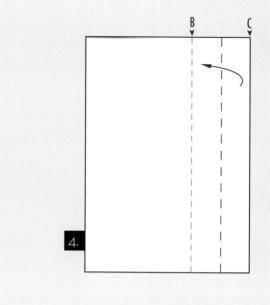

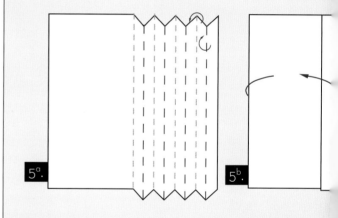

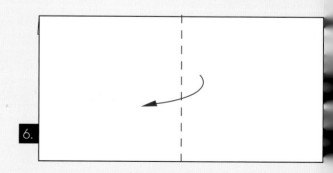

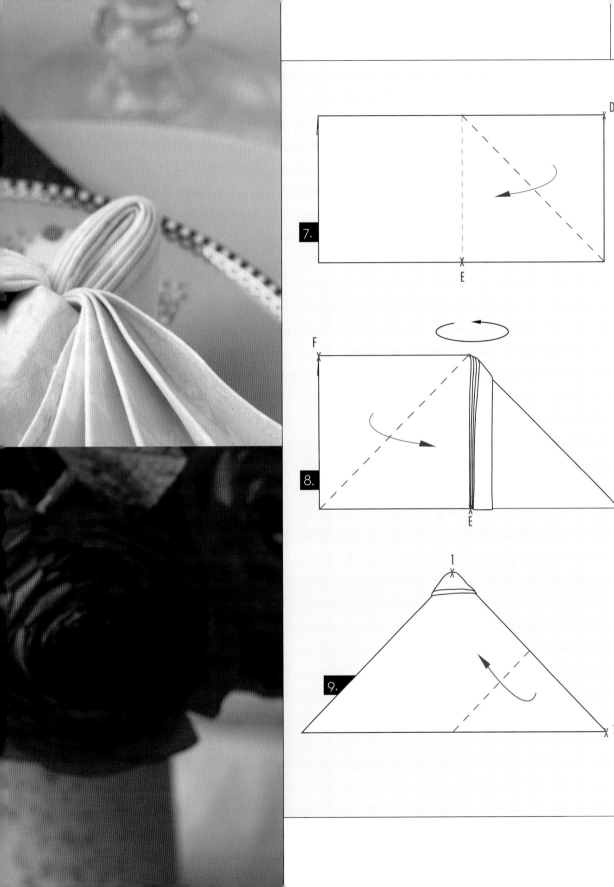

10.

Fold the bottom left-hand corner to the top of the napkin along the dashed red line, bringing point 3 to point 1.
Iron to press the fold.

11.

Fold the right-hand part of the napkin downwards (top layer) along the dashed red line, bringing point 4 to point 5.

12.

Fold the left-hand part of the napkin downwards (top layer) along the dashed red line, bringing point 6 to point 7.

13.

Take corners 6 and 4 and carefully unfold them by pulling gently to the sides.

14.

Push corner 8 inwards between the two layers of fabric. Line up the edges marked in blue. Because of the creases you made earlier, the rest of the section will sit in place naturally.

15.

Repeat on the left-hand side (shaded area). Push corner 9 inwards between the two layers of fabric. Line up the edges marked in blue.

16.

Fold the right-hand corner to the centre of the napkin along the dashed red line. Iron to press the fold.

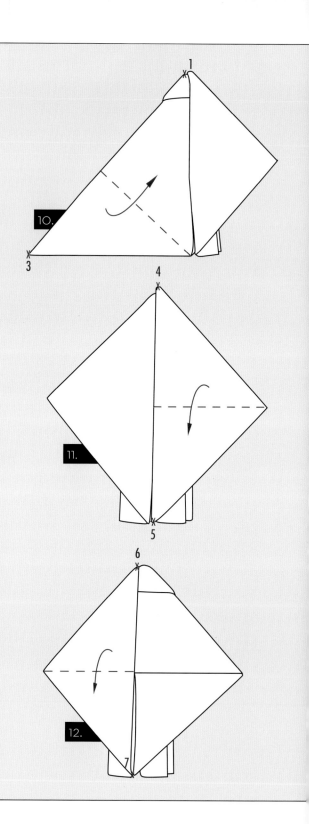

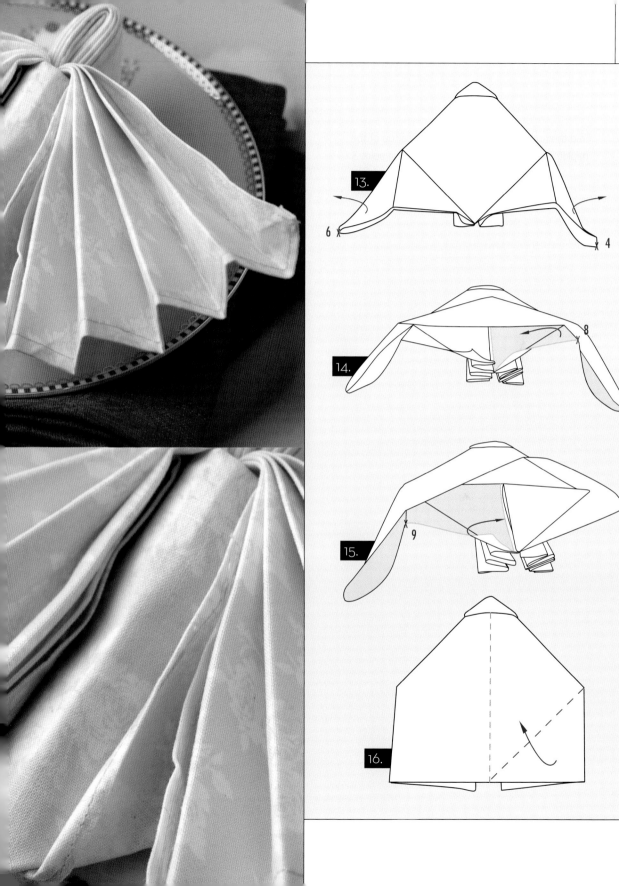

17.

Repeat the previous step with the left-hand corner, folding it to the centre of the napkin along the dashed red line. Iron to press the fold.

18.

Fold the point of the napkin downwards along the dashed red line.

19.

Fold the top layer of the napkin (shaded area) in half upwards along the dashed red line. Iron to press the fold.

20.

Fold the right-hand point of the napkin to the centre. Slip the end of it under the shaded part. Push gently to tuck it in.

21.

Repeat with the left-hand point. Fold to the middle of the napkin. Slip the end of it under the shaded part. Push gently to tuck it in.

22.

Flip the napkin over. Spread the butterfly's wings.

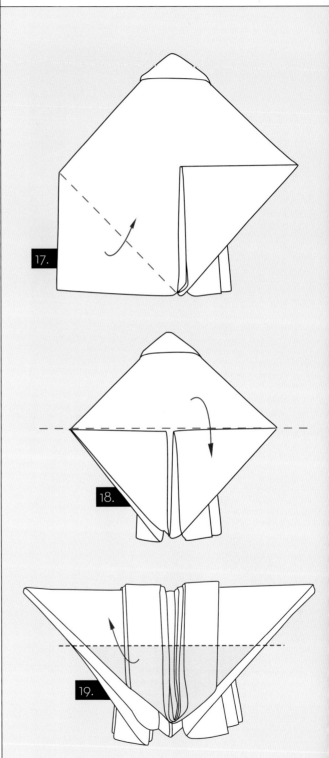

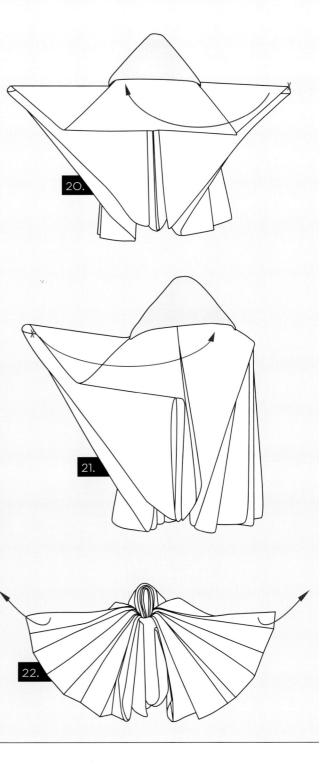

20.

21.

22.

Acanthus leaf

1.

Lay a square napkin on the work surface, wrong side up. Fold in half diagonally.

2.

Fold this triangle into accordion pleats. Each pleat should be around 2cm (1in) wide. Alternate valley folds (dashed red lines) with mountain folds (dashed blue lines). Iron each fold.

3.

Once the whole napkin is pleated, pinch the base firmly and wrap a strand of matching wool (or any other yarn) around the napkin to secure in place. Knot.

4.

Open out the pleats carefully to create the final flower shape.

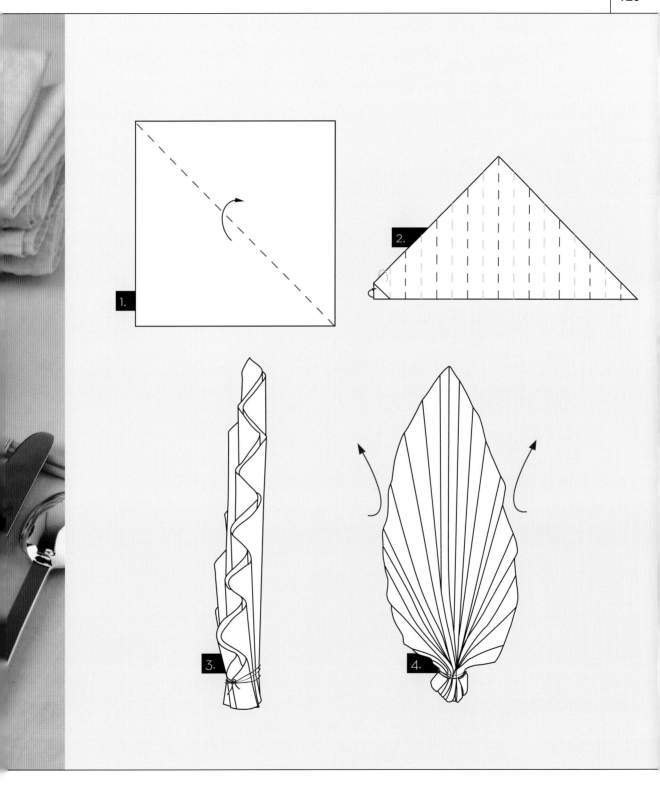

City chic

Special delivery

1.

Lay a square napkin on the work surface, wrong side up. Fold in half vertically, following the dashed red line. Iron to mark the fold. Unfold. Fold in half horizontally, following the dashed blue line. Iron and then unfold. You will use these creases as guides later.

2.

Fold the left-hand quarter (A) and the right-hand quarter (B) to the centre of the napkin (C) along the dashed red lines. Spray with starch and iron to press the folds.

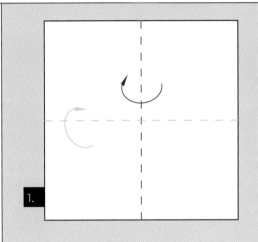

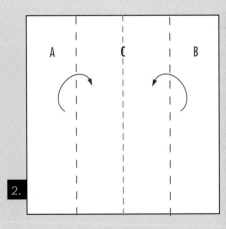

3.

Fold the top quarter (D) and the bottom quarter (F) to the centre of the napkin (E) along the dashed red lines. Iron to mark the folds, then unfold. These horizontal creases will act as guides in the later stages.

4.

Fold the top right-hand corner (1) of the napkin to the middle (C) along the dashed red line. Iron to press the fold.

5.

Fold the top left-hand corner (2) to the middle (C) of the napkin along the dashed red line. Iron to press the fold.

6.

Fold the bottom quarter of the napkin to the middle using the creases that you made previously, aligning the red lines. Iron.

7.

Fold the bottom quarter of the napkin again, aligning the red lines. Iron.

8.

Fold the point of the napkin downwards along the dashed red line to form the envelope. Iron.

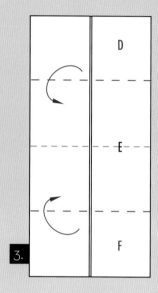

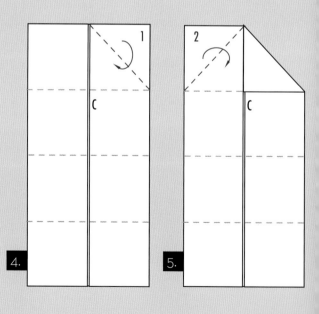

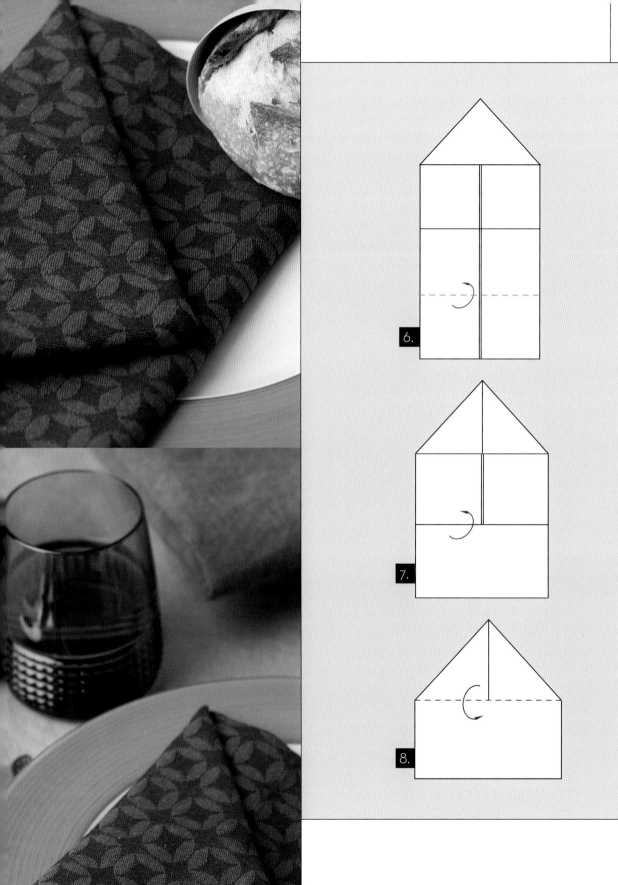

6.

7.

8.

Open book

1.
Lay a square napkin on the work surface, wrong side up. Fold in half horizontally following the dashed red line. Iron to mark the fold, then unfold again.

2.
Fold the bottom of the napkin up to the centre along the dashed red line, aligning edge A with the central crease. Iron to press the fold.

3.
Repeat this step with the top of the napkin. Align edge B with the central crease, folding along the dashed red line. Iron to press the fold.

4.
Fold the napkin in half horizontally along the dashed red line. Iron to press the fold.

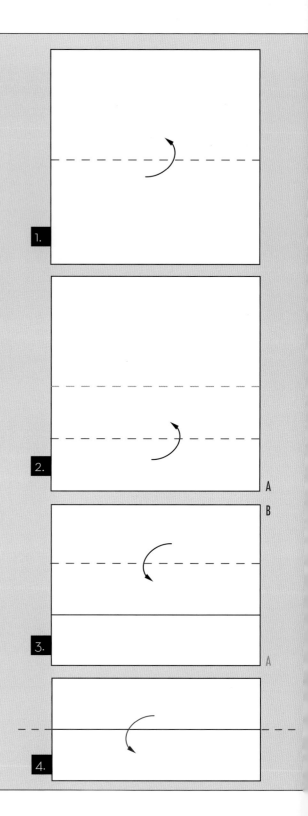

5.

Fold in half vertically along the dashed red line. Iron to mark the fold.

6.

Fold the right-hand third inwards. Fold just the top layer, following the dashed red line. Iron to press the fold.

7.

Do the same with the right-hand third of the bottom layer of the napkin, folding it behind. Iron to press the fold.

8.

Open out the napkin. Fold the right-hand third of the napkin inwards along the dashed red line, aligning the right-hand edge with the central crease. Iron the fold.

9.

Repeat this step on the left-hand third of the napkin, folding it inwards along the dashed red line, aligning the left-hand edge with the central crease. Iron the fold.

10.

a) Push corner A upwards, between the two layers of fabric. b) Flatten it to form a triangle. Fold the left-hand layer of the fabric (shaded area) over the right.

11.

a) Repeat with the left-hand page. a) Push corner B upwards, between the two layers of fabric. b) Flatten it to form a triangle. Fold the right-hand layer of the fabric (shaded area) over the left.

12.

Adjust the folds so they sit at the same angles on each side.

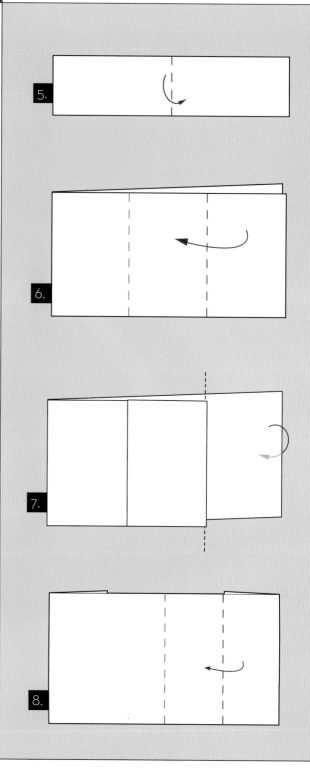

Pocket square

1.

Lay a square napkin on your work surface, wrong side up. Fold in half diagonally. Rotate the napkin so the top of the triangle points upwards. Iron to press the fold.

Note: This project works best with a thin napkin that is patterned on both sides. Spray starch regularly to make sure it holds its shape. If you want a smaller pocket, fold the napkin into four before you begin.
It is important that you have a square to begin with.

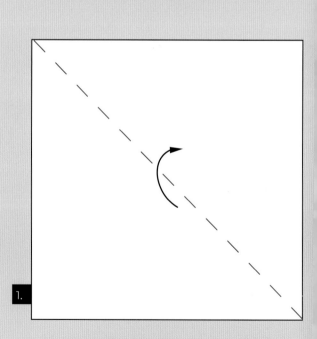

1.

2.

Fold the top layer of the napkin along the dashed line, bringing the top point (A) to the lower edge of the triangle. Iron to mark the fold. Unfold. The point where this fold intersects with the right-hand side of triangle will be called C. This crease will act as a useful guide in the following step.

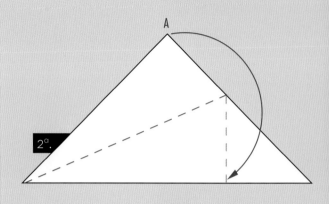

3.

Bring the bottom left-hand corner (B) to point C, folding along the dashed red line.

4.

Bring the bottom right-hand corner (D) to the left-hand edge of the triangle at point E, folding along the dashed red line. Iron.

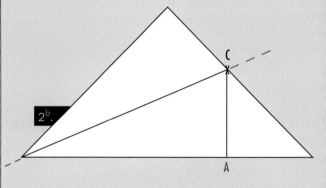

5.

Fold the top point of the triangle downwards (top layer only).

6.

Fold the remaining point backwards. Slip your hand inside to open the pocket out and give it volume.

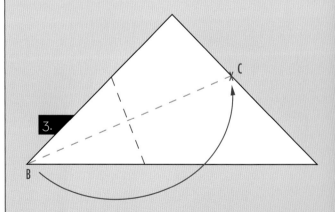

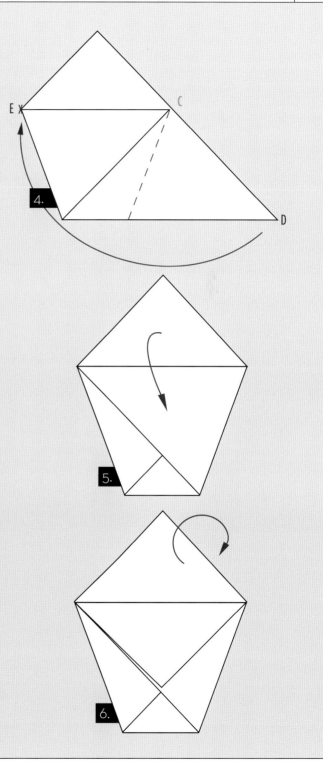

Dressed for dinner

1.
Lay a square (or rectangular) napkin on your work surface, wrong side up. Fold in half horizontally following the dashed red line. Spray with a little starch and iron to press the fold.

2.
Fold the top layer of the napkin in half horizontally, following the dashed red line. Iron to mark the fold.

3.
Fold in half horizontally once again, following the dashed red line. Iron to mark the fold. Unfold. These creases will act as guides subsequently.

4.
Fold the first layer of the napkin, aligning edge 1 and crease 4 which you made previously (dashed blue line). Iron to press the fold.

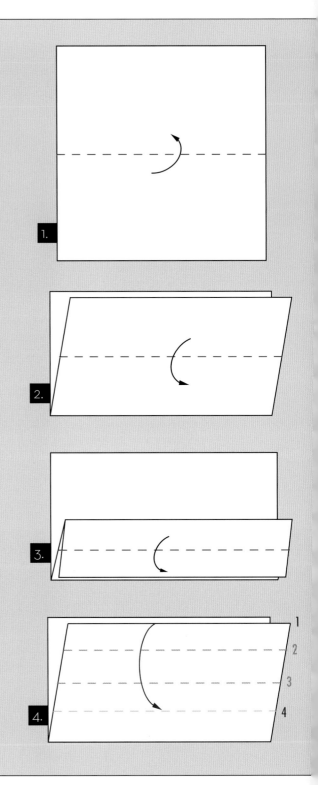

5.

Fold the back layer of the napkin (shaded area), aligning edge 5 with crease 2 which you made previously (dashed blue line). Iron to mark the fold.

6.

Fold in half vertically, following the dashed red line. Spray lightly with starch and iron again.

7.

Fold the right-hand third of the top layer of the napkin to the left along the dashed red line. Iron to press the fold.

8.

Do the same with the right-hand third of the bottom layer of the napkin (shaded area), folding it behind. Iron to mark the fold.

9.

Open out the napkin. Fold the right-hand third of the napkin inwards along the dashed red line, aligning the right-hand edge with the central crease. Iron to press the fold.

10.

Fold the left-hand third of the napkin inwards along the dashed red line, aligning the left-hand edge with the central crease. Iron to press the fold.

11.

Rotate the napkin 180° so the pockets are facing in the right direction. Slip in the menu and table place name card.

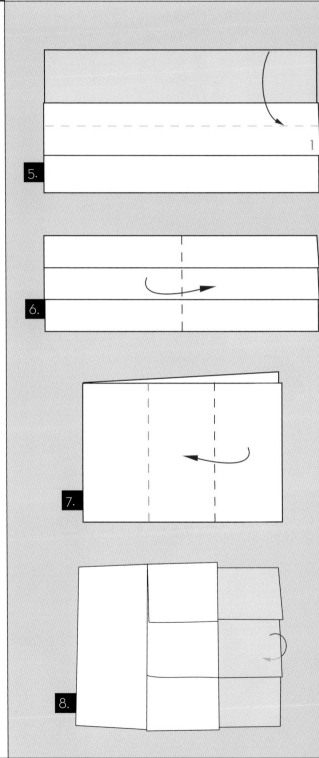

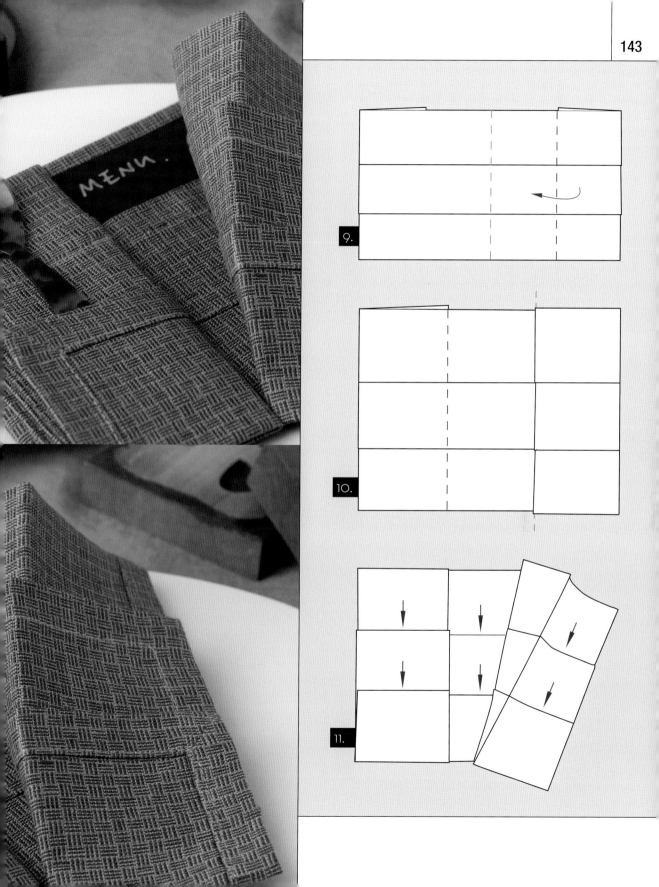

9.

10.

11.

Business lunch

1.
Lay a square napkin on the work surface, wrong side up. Fold up the bottom third of the napkin along the dashed red lines, aligning edge D with line B. Iron the fold.

2.
Fold the top third of the napkin down, aligning edge A with edge C. Iron the fold.

3.
Make a fold along the top layer of the napkin approximately 2cm (1in) wide, then refold several times until you reach the middle of the napkin. Iron the napkin, then flip over.

4.
Fold the left-hand edge of the napkin inwards to make a flap approximately 6cm (2½in) wide. Refold this flap several times, following the dashed red lines.

5.
Iron the napkin again. If the right-hand edge protrudes slightly, fold it inside the napkin.

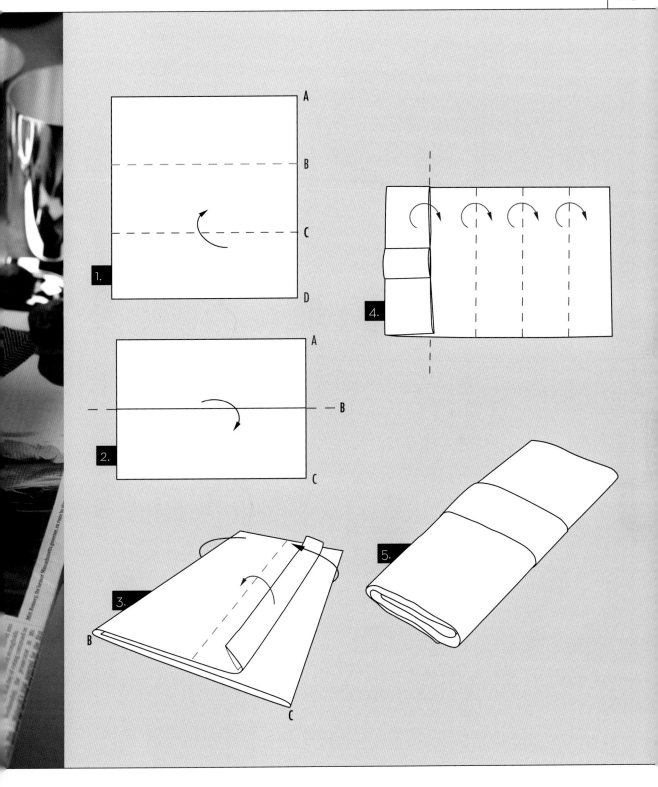

Sea air

Small fry

1.
Lay a square napkin on the work surface, wrong side up. Fold a band of around 2cm (1in) to the back of the napkin, following the dashed red line. Iron to press the fold.

2.
Fold the napkin in half vertically along the dashed red line. Iron to press the fold.

3.
Fold the napkin in half horizontally along the dashed red line. Iron to mark the fold.

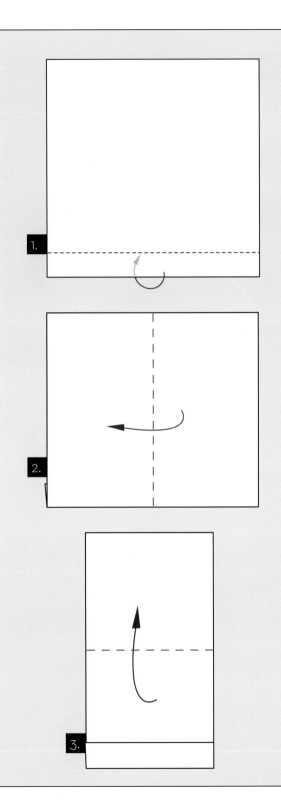

4.
Fold the napkin in half vertically along the dashed red line. Iron to mark the fold, then unfold again. This crease will act as a guide.

5.
Fold the bottom right-hand corner to the centre, along the dashed red line. Iron to mark the fold, then unfold again.

6.
Push corner A inwards. Following the creases made previously, it will open naturally into a triangle. Flatten it out with the iron. Then fold the shaded area to the right.

7.
Fold the bottom left-hand corner to the centre along the dashed red line. Iron to mark the fold, then unfold again.

8.
Push corner B inwards. Following the creases made previously, it will open naturally into a triangle. Flatten it out with the iron. Then fold the shaded area to the left.

9.
Flip the napkin over. Following the dashed line, fold the top layer of the fabric downwards.

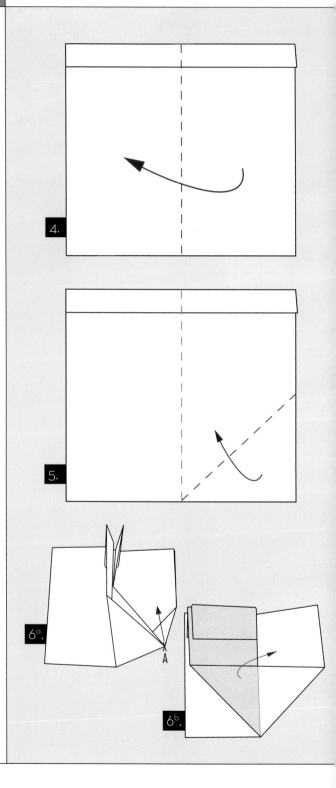

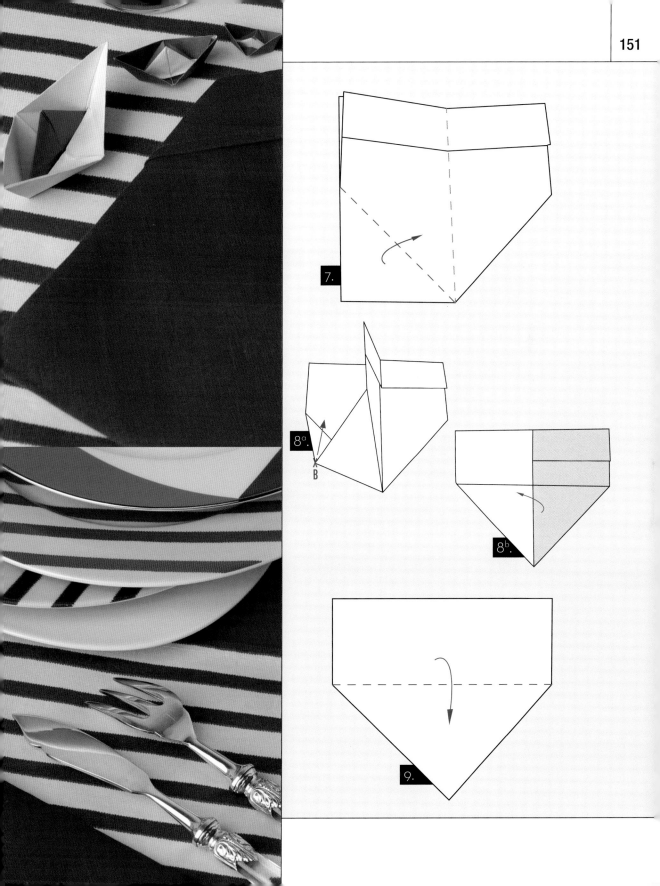

7.

8ª.

A

B

8ᵇ.

9.

10.
By folding along the dashed line, bring edge E to point F.

11.
By folding along the dashed line, bring edge G to point F.

12.
Fold the top right-hand corner along the dashed line and align the edges marked in blue.

13.
Repeat the previous step with the left-hand corner, folding along the dashed line and aligning the edges marked in blue.

14.
Spray with starch. Iron to press the folds. Flip the napkin over.

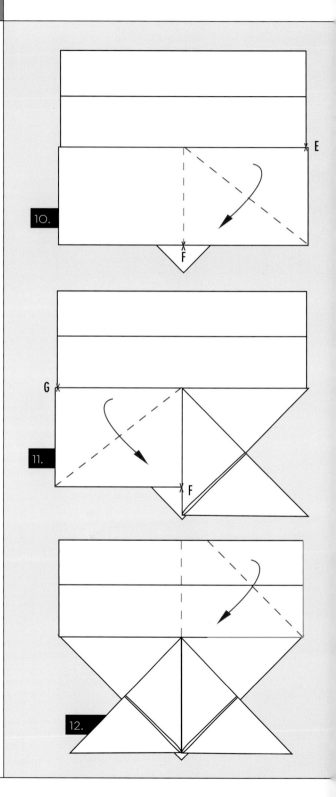

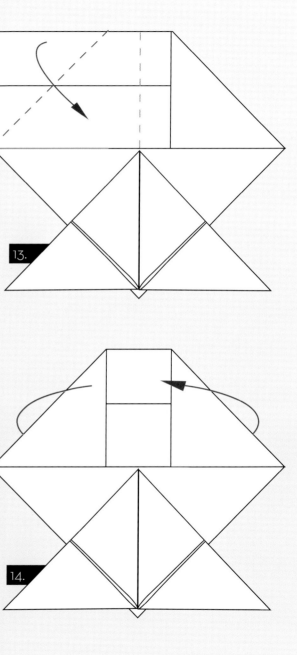

13.

14.

Double knot

1.

Lay a square napkin on the work surface, wrong side up. Fold in half horizontally along the dashed red line. Spray with starch. Iron to press the fold.

2.

Fold the napkin in half vertically along the dashed line, bringing the right-hand side (B) over the left-hand side (A). Spray lightly with starch. Iron the fold.

3.

Fold the right- and left-hand thirds of the napkin inwards. Flip over.

4.

To make the 'napkin ring', use some hemp twine that is 6mm (¼in) in diameter and approximately 50cm (20in) in length. Fold it in half, then follow the diagrams to make a double figure-of-eight knot. Position the knot in the centre of the napkin. Slip the ends through the loop.

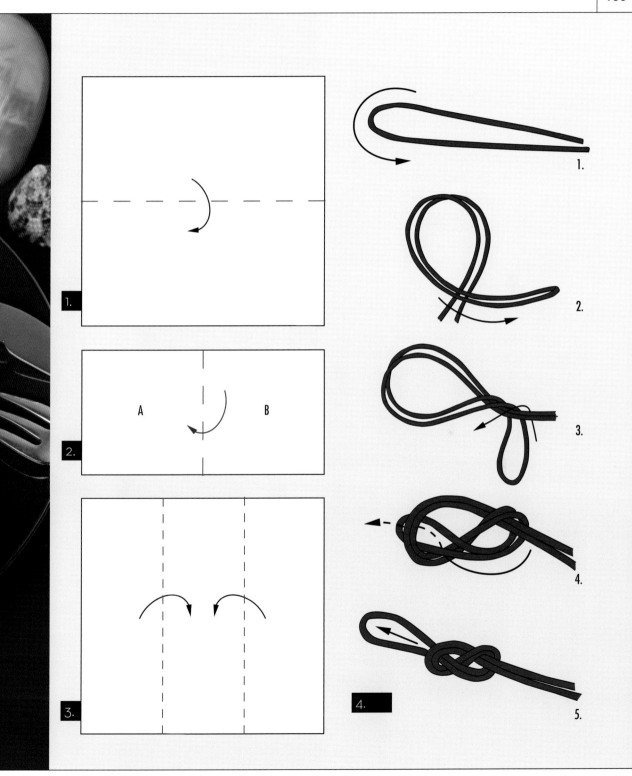

1.

2.

A   B

3.

4.

1.

2.

3.

4.

5.

Hoist the flag

1.
Lay a square napkin on the work surface, wrong side up. Fold in half horizontally following the dashed red line. Make sure that the opening is facing you. Spray with starch. Iron to mark the fold.

2.
Bring point A at the top right-hand corner to point B in the middle of the base of the triangle, folding along the dashed red line. Iron to press the fold.

3.
Repeat the previous step with the left-hand corner (C), bringing point C to point B by folding along the dashed red line. Iron to press the fold.

4.
Fold this triangle in half vertically, bringing point 2 to point 1 by folding along the dashed red line.

5.
Stand the napkin up as shown in the diagram.

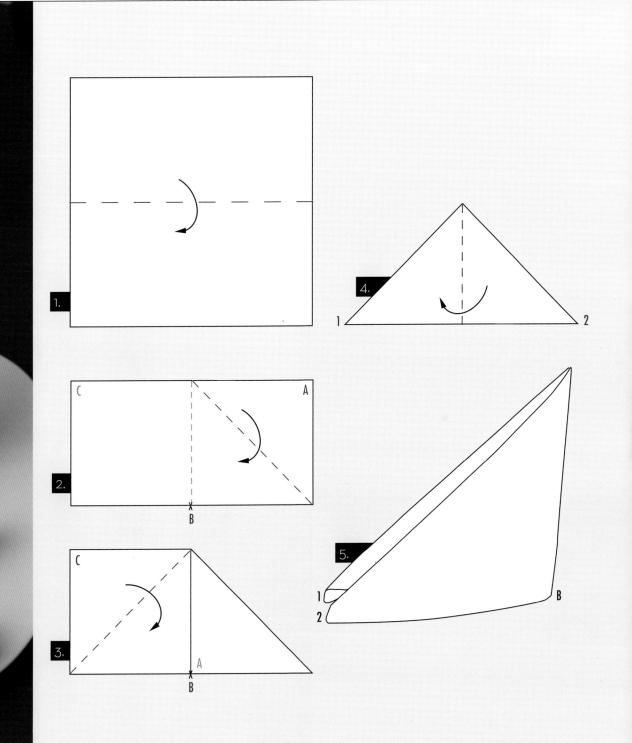

157

Ahoy there!

1.
Lay a square napkin on the work surface, wrong side up. Fold in half diagonally. Rotate the napkin so the top of the triangle points upwards. Iron to press the fold.

2.
Fold the point of the napkin downwards, bringing point A to point B by folding along the dashed red line. Iron to press the fold.

3.
Fold the napkin in half horizontally, following the dashed red line. Iron to press the fold.

4.
Repeat this step again, folding the napkin in half horizontally along the dashed red line. Iron to press the fold.

5.
Holding on to the rolled napkin carefully so that it does not come undone, tie a knot in the middle.

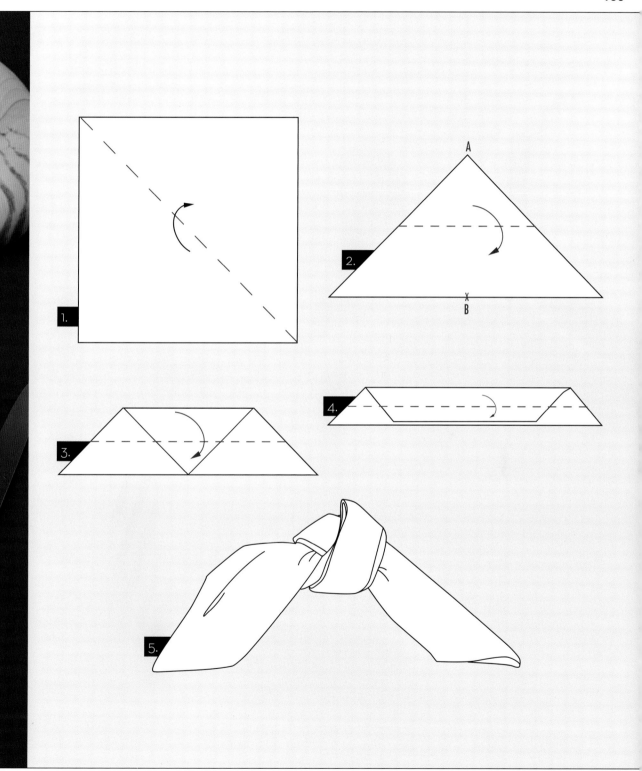

ACKNOWLEDGEMENTS

THANKS TO:

Marie Dáage; Dîners en ville; Magna Carta; Secret maison; Comptoir de famille; Mis en demeure; Sabre; Bougies la Française; Jardins d'Ulysse; Society; BHV; Jardins imaginaires; Kimonoya; Jars; Alessi.

Napkins add a touch of elegance and sophistication to
your dining table and this book is a wonderful source of
inspiration to help you decorate and customize your home
with taste and creativity. Napkins are functional as well as
decorative, and there are 40 lovely designs to choose from,
including a pleated rectangle, a leaf, a flower and a knot.
Each napkin design is explained through clear, step-by-step
instructions and illustrations. There are folds to suit every
occasion from a smart dinner party to a family barbecue,
weddings, picnics and more. Gain all the skills, techniques
and expertise you need to create stunning, contemporary
table decorations to a professional standard.

The world's finest art and craft books
www.searchpress.com

UK £12.99/US $19.95/CAN $23.95
ISBN 978-1-78221-761-9